Quick, Said the Bird

Quick, Said the Bird

Williams, Eliot, Moore, and the Spoken Word

RICHARD SWIGG

UNIVERSITY OF IOWA PRESS   IOWA CITY

University of Iowa Press, Iowa City 52242
Copyright © 2012 by the University of Iowa Press
www.uiowapress.org
Printed in the United States of America

Design by Omega Clay

The University of Iowa Press is a member of Green Press Initiative
and is committed to preserving natural resources.

Printed on acid-free paper

Library of Congress Cataloging-in-Publication Data
Swigg, Richard, 1938–
Quick, said the bird: Williams, Eliot, Moore, and the spoken word
/ Richard Swigg.
   p. cm.
Includes bibliographical references and index.
ISBN-13: 978-1-60938-079-3 (pbk)
ISBN-10: 1-60938-079-7 (pbk)
1. American poetry—20th century—History and criticism. 2. Oral
interpretation of poetry. 3. Williams, William Carlos, 1883–1963—
Criticism and interpretation. 4. Eliot, T. S. (Thomas Stearns),
1888–1965—Criticism and interpretation. 5. Moore, Marianne,
1887–1972—Criticism and interpretation. I. Title.
PS323.5.S95 2012
811′.509—dc23 2011039507

For Charles Tomlinson

CONTENTS

ACKNOWLEDGMENTS

My special thanks must go to Emily Mitchell Wallace, eminent bibliographer of William Carlos Williams. Her unflinching support and advice have been especially valuable. I am also indebted to Danny Lawrence, John Wheatcroft, and Richard Warren at the Yale Historical Recordings Collection.

ABBREVIATIONS

CWP1	*The Collected Poems of William Carlos Williams I*
CWP2	*The Collected Poems of William Carlos Williams II*
CPP	*T. S. Eliot: The Complete Poems and Plays*
IMH	*Inventions of the March Hare*
PMM	*The Poems of Marianne Moore*
OB	*Observations*

INTRODUCTION

When Williams said "It's all in / the sound," or when Eliot hailed the invigorating force of the "auditory imagination," or when Moore applauded "the
clatter and true sound" of Williams's verse while catching the "differentiated,
kindred sounds" at work in Eliot's,[1] each poet invoked the dimension that essentially bound them together. Deeper than any quarrel—such as Williams's
denunciation of Eliot's *The Waste Land* for allegedly betraying native ground
and idiom—the acoustics of all three poets take us directly to the linkages,
kinships, and inter-illuminations of a major twentieth-century literary relationship. Outsiders in their home terrain yet reaching back to their own
American vocal identity, they embody an especially unique lineage which I
here seek to trace from their first significant work (1909–1918) to the 1960s.

Amongst the three, Eliot may seem incongruous. Should not this expatriate be regarded as nearer to Pound, vital at key moments in the writing
of the many-voiced *Waste Land*? Yet in Eliot's estrangement from his own
country and the spoken new distinctiveness that he gains thereby, he actually has less affinity with Pound, the more avowed cultural exile, than with
Williams and Moore: all three closer still to those other contemporaries of
the vocalized word who also stand apart from an accepted homeground consciousness, though in their case by reason of racial history. It is notable that
when Moore in "Black Earth" implicitly declared her own independence as
a poetic animal from the literary scene that had rejected her, Pound's mis-
taken assumption about her ("are you a jet black Ethiopian Othello-hued.
. . ?")[2] accidentally touched upon the circumstance from which ensued a
parallel movement of literary separateness in the 1920s, exemplified in particular by Zora Neale Hurston, Jean Toomer, and Langston Hughes. This, to
Houston Baker's ears, is a black modernism so distant from Eliot's kind that
it "consists, finally, not in tumbling towers or bursts in the violet air, but in a
sounding renaissancism," a vocalized "guerilla" counterattack against "white
control and suppositions."[3] But Philipp Schweighauser, who listens instead to
the shared acoustics of black and white in the prose of Hurston and Dos Pas-
sos, finds Toomer's disruptive mixture of poetry, drama, and prose in *Cane* to
have much in common with the "fragmentation and unresolved tensions" of
"Anglo-Saxon modernisms"[4]—a link that Michael North takes further in *The
Dialect of Modernism* by tying the 1923 *Cane* more closely to Williams's *Spring
and All* in the same year, as well as making the larger assertion that Eliot and

Williams turned their poetry "black," in linguistic racial disguise, so that they could rebel against Anglophilia and tradition.

This seems to me a claim that needs to be examined and qualified later. More immediately, however, let me insist on the importance of not blurring one modernism by another. Williams, Eliot, and Moore have a singular distinction, when discussed in relation to one another, which should no more be lost to auditory view than that displayed by the writers of the black renaissance. If the latter deserve the attention of a sharpened ear, so does the verse of struggle, mishap, and achievement in this particular modernist kinship. But in tracking its varied course and thereby adding to an already large critical discussion,[5] I am working in a way that has been largely neglected by broader commentaries. That is, I seek to render the *speaking* voice of the printed text—one that has to be deduced from the marks on the page, is constructed out loud, stays subject to the changing pace and the needs of breath-control, emphases, and enunciation, then possibly ends a verse sequence (an unfolding temporal sequence, not static fragments) in a way that is totally different from the beginning. It is an interpretation of the lines by performance—a discovery of meaning's unexpected contours by lips, tongue, and throat—that can often revise the mind's interpretation of a poem that has been largely known through silent reading.

This way of discussing the poetry is therefore markedly different from the kind of commentary which keeps "voice" in poetry at a generalized, unspoken distance, or makes the arrangement of words on the page superior to audible utterance—the bias toward *écriture* over *parole* which Henry Sayre openly displays when discussing Williams,[6] and to which Stephen Cushman more implicitly adheres when he assumes that the author of "Seafarer," in his search for "auditory justification," is so regulated by the visual "pictogram" of his text that he should have stopped at line-endings when recording the poem.[7] Williams, by contrast, with his "liking . . . for an unimpeded thrust right through the poem from the beginning to end, without regard to formal arrangements,"[8] shows no sympathy for the idea that visual organization is the ruling principle that a vocal reading is simply there to endorse. Even so, the over-visual bias in criticism persists.[9] Existing as the "sight-dominance" described by Walter Ong, from the invention of the printing press onward, when greater legibility of texts made for rapid, silent reading,[10] it is also there in the long history of "visualism" traced by Don Ihde from Plato to Descartes and Locke, when the eye of reason and "disembodied . . . 'pure' acts of the mind"[11] were exalted above perceptual, sense-bound experience. But in escaping the prejudice of sight over sound, one should not go to the other extreme, as Williams does in minimizing the importance of the textual "formal arrangements." They matter as crucially as the vocal thrust he describes: a clear pointer to what he shares with Eliot and Moore in the spoken drive of the poetry, the forward-moving utterance tensed against by the discipline of the eye-read text, as voice and vision work together in vital inter-reaction. Indeed, I would go further in suggesting that the visual arrangement, whether this takes the form of line-breaks, spacings, indentings, the isolating of words, or the shape of verse-paragraphs and stanza-blocks, is only seen in its true function and given its rightful, key place alongside the acoustics when the spoken reading of the poem is raised from secondary to primary importance.

Clearly it has that importance in the poets' own recordings of their work. Eliot began in 1933 with a series of readings for Harvard's Poetry Room, and was recorded in England and America until the 1950s. But it is his virtually unknown recording of *The Waste Land*, made at Columbia University in 1933, which shows especially how the ear can be directed to major qualities in the text—*in* it, not added by spoken performance—which the eye often overlooks. For it is here that his passionate yet text-justified account of the poem runs counter to the notion of it as a hymn to sterile defeat, ameliorated by vegetation rites and anthropology. Down on the acoustic ground one also cannot escape—despite Eliot's own attempt to impose an overarching unity by means of the tarot cards and the supposedly all-inclusive Tiresias—the disparate sounds of the verse's urgent striving, moment by moment, out of silence and aridity. Moreover, the remarkable energy of this spoken version, as distinct from his better known postwar reading, puts it alongside the springy delivery or amazingly fast-paced style which Williams could achieve in the recordings he made from 1942 to 1962, and which I subsequently published as a collection.[12] Moore also has a long recording history, which begins with her reading "Virginia Britannia" and other poems at City College of New York in 1941, and ends, it would seem, with the reading of later work at the University of Texas in 1968. But her career as a recorded reader, where a languid delivery is often at odds with the enunciating dexterity required by the poems, more starkly brings into question any undue critical dependence on the poets' recordings. Whatever the benefits of hearing a good, spoken version, where it occurs—a stimulus which I gladly acknowledge at relevant moments throughout—the evidence of disc or tape cannot be for me the sole guide to the poems' acoustic possibilities. I am dealing here, after all, with a range of poems that the authors never recorded, as well as those they did, and sometimes (this includes Williams and Eliot, not just Moore) less than satisfactorily.

Therefore, in keeping a sympathetic yet critical relationship to the recordings, while certainly not offering a comparison of the poets as readers of their own work, I find overall that the surest way forward is to remain an independent vocal reader of the verse. Attempting this, I differ from Eric Griffiths when he suggests that the speaking of poetry aloud is secondary to the poet's unutterable, silent self, and that voicing turns the indeterminateness of the text ("writing is an inherently ambiguous notation")[13] into an arbitrary fixity. In contrast, I find it is better to risk one's own imperfections as reader—to hazard an entry into the auditory texture, and thus vocally possess a poem in order, at a deeper level, to be possessed *by* it—than to keep an ideal reading solely in the mind, untethered by any particular voicing and therefore, unhearably, nowhere. On the other hand, I am not drawn to the strict rendering of modernist poems by machine-made notation recommended by Charles Olson when he observes in Williams, Cummings, and Pound the use of the typewriter as "a scoring to [the poet's] composing, as a script to its vocalization."[14] This is to systematize what Pound less rigidly claims when he says that "ALL typographic dispositions, placing of words *on* the page, is intended to facilitate the reader's intonation, whether he be reading silently to self or aloud to friends."[15] So, though the poetic text is not an over-rigid score, and though Moore, Eliot, and Williams can play the voice *against* "typographic dispositions," the read-aloud words on the page provide the clue not just to the intonation but to the vital forward movement of the poem, by syntax or sequential impetus: what I describe in this book, together with other acoustic features, by the language of metrics, rhyme, rhythm, assonance, alliteration, aspirates, syllabic emphases, and speech-sounds, as well as by a wider linguistic portrayal that invokes cries, whispers, leaps, thrusts, sinkings, resurgences, lingerings or rapped-out curtness.

A poem's onward movement can therefore be descriptively tracked, whether one is following it through the breakups of an Eliot paragraph, Williams's word-block divisions, or, as in the case of Moore, through the sound of a stanza that feigns quietness. In her unrecorded early poem, "To Be Liked by You Would Be a Calamity" (1916) a silent dignity is kept by not replying in kind to the words of a boor: "I can but put my weapon up and / Bow you out" (OB, 37). Her tactic, however, belongs to a poetry of battle which, as Ellen Levy remarks, she "unleashed on a seemingly hostile literary world at a crucial point in her career."[16] For though she apparently yields to speechless surrender, the poem actually drives forward with the acoustics of counterattack:

> Let unsheathed gesticulation be the steel
>   Your courtesy must meet,
>   Since in your hearing words are mute, which to my senses
>   Are a shout.

Here the poet's "unsh*ea*thed ges*t*iculation" is the "*steel*" that "must m*ee*t," with deadly decorum, and with a syntactic, continuous lunge, the barbarous "courtesy" of one deaf to such sounds. For though in her opponent's hearing her "words are mute," a subversively heard anger, clashing "mute" against "meet," builds from that dissonance—with "my *senses*" emphatically differentiated from "your hearing" across the length of a penultimate four-stress line—the words that "Are," in sudden brevity, "a sh*out*": extra-loud in the rhyme with "Bow you out," but preserving the pseudo-silence of its decorous poise.

One may similarly elicit and describe the acoustic impetus of a poem by Williams, again without the need of a recording. For though his "Young Sycamore" (1930) was actually taped twenty years later, the recording does less than justice to the urgency and pace which is demanded of the speaker from the very beginning:

> I must tell you
> this young tree
> whose round and firm trunk
> between the wet
>
> pavement and the gutter
> (where water
> is trickling) rises
> bodily
>
> into the air with
> one undulant
> thrust ... (CWP1, 266)

According to J. Hillis Miller, this is a poem "without dramatic action" which "takes place in a single moment."[17] But what he imagines as an instant seizing of the subject is actually a line-by-line revelation—if one *speaks* the poem, that is—whose timebound steps are not to be outsoared, despite the urgency that Williams brought to its rewriting. What once began more hesitantly ("I feel that I must")[18] now starts with the excited impulsiveness of "I must tell you" which pairs on the page more trimly, and in speech more closely (*"you"* nearer *"young"*), with "this young tree." The spoken impetus of a verbal tree is on the move, as the sentence takes in all those hard-edged *t*'s (tell, tree, trunk, between, wet pavement, gutter, trickling), with an unbroken force magnified by the stark stanza-break it must cross between "wet" and "pavement." Indeed, the very smallness of the textual blocks, and the arbitrary look of their line-breaks, intensify the sense of speech's continuous, unstoppable onwardness, as it pushes past obstructions: "between the wet // pavement and the gutter" ("where," in another adverbial impediment, "wa*ter*" clings to the sound of "gu*tter*" in a trickling diversion of the sentence). Across those barriers and despite the visual cuttings-in (yet *because* of them) the trunk of tree and statement "rises / bodily"—free at last—"into the air" on the upsurge that keeps its sinuous shape with a continuity of *un*'s and *u* in "one undulant / thrust."

By contrast, the segments of different voices in *The Waste Land* seem to offer no such unbroken continuity: that is, if never heard. But if a vocal reading is tried, acoustic linkages open up which complement, without excessive reliance upon, Eliot's own notable recording. For his words alone offer the means and the prompting to find the connective path which does in fact lead through a sequence of apparent fragmentation. Hence in "The Burial of the Dead," as the text breaks off from the desert prophet's words, "I will show you fear in a handful of dust," and cuts to the sailor's song from *Tristan und Isolde*, isolated on the page—

> *Frisch weht der Wind*
> *Der Heimat zu*
> *Mein Irisch Kind*
> *Wo weilest du?* (CPP, 30)

—one observes, as speaker, how the low-pitched threat to "you" and the harsh English consonants ("han*d*ful of *dust*") are transformed (the dust blown away) by the *t*-sharp German freshness of "Frisch weh*t* der Win*d*" and the intonationally upward reach of the question—the singer high on his ship—toward a longed for, absent "du." "You," the next word, carries the impetus forward, but now in the wistful, quieter English that the strong German yearning has vocally highlighted: not the language of a distant Irish child but that of a Hyacinth girl, reaching out across another divide ("You gave me Hyacinths first a year ago") to a lover whose mute thought-answer seems provoked, in its jaggedness, by her fluent innocence: "—Yet [*haltingly*] when we came back, [*pause*] late, from the hyacinth garden . . . I could not [*in line-break hesitancy*] Speak." Saying that, however, one must equally abide by the modulation of the style into rhythmic smoothness when he goes on to declare he is "neither / Living nor dead . . . Looking into the heart of light, the silence": an English fluency that again provokes a staccato reply with "Oed' und leer das Meer." But if the German gutturals offer a last *liebestod* cry to Wagner's Tristan and all separated lovers, they equally prepare the voice for a leap to the jerky sprightliness which starts the next paragraph: "Madame Sosostris, famous clairvoyante," curtly Frenchified in Eliot's recording as "clair*vw*yonte."

So one might trace the different yet shared ways in which individual passages sequentially unfold. But this book is also concerned with the broader continuities that Eliot, Moore, and Williams hold in common. It is, after all, by the adoption of a bold, outgoing role as a speaker that each first emerged into maturity. By this, they reached beyond the romantic ego, phantoms, solitary introspection, or the over-defensive self to a sounded world—"sounded," that is, in terms of uttering or addressing a circumambient scene of people, animals, objects, or locality; but also "sounded" in the sense of depths or shallows plumbed, of verbal or emotional resonances sharpened as words relate more keenly to the world. It is a relation that, when we hear it, connects the Eliot of internationalism and the Williams who would champion the "American idiom": one poet amidst the postwar breakages of Europe, re-gathering history's echoes into a greater, energized sound; the other poet creating again and again a focused dignity out of the linguistic scraps, unuttered pieces, and diffuse demeanings of his own unabandoned country. In the making of extraordinary congruences there also stands the other acoustic adventurer, Moore, with her disparate poetic assemblages and her clustering together of different levels of American speech in "Those Various Scalpels"—with "impeccable skill," Eliot sees, as if he too stands ironically apart from what he calls an "uneasy language of stereotypes."[19] Yet she, with her versatile animal sense (whether animality means fauna, flora, hybrids, or the animated solidities of the pluralistic world) brings into auditory view not just the disparate particulars which she also enjoyed in Williams's verse but the striving by herself and fellow-outsiders toward a nonhuman yet essentially native utterance.

It is the keen-edged life tracked as much by Moore in a frigate pelican, a Virginian mockingbird, or the eagles of Mount Rainier as it is by Williams following through the gymnastics of starlings in the wind, a bird winging down to its watery image, or the notes of a redbreast by the Passaic Falls: all instances of a poetic outreach into the zestfully unsilenced which still persists in the later Eliot's call, "Quick, said the bird," as the thrush of an English garden points the acoustic memory back to the cries of the Philomela nightingale or the water-dripping song of the North American hermit-thrush in *The Waste Land.* To be "quick" here is not necessarily to be speedy but to tease open the bounds of the narrow self—eschewing, as do Moore and Williams, the comforts of an oceanic spread for the expanded yet tighter aims of alacrity and acuity. It is quickening for all three poets with the sense of exceptional vivifying: the word swooping to utterance with an accuracy and an energy that also provides a standard of achievement. By its measure in this book I have therefore concentrated on areas of special distinction. Hence the compressive mastery of Williams's short-line verse receives the kind of attention that the mythic scope of *Paterson* does not, while emphasis falls on *The Waste Land* and other Eliot poems, but notably less so on the extent of *Four Quartets.* By the same principle, I have given little space to Moore's post-1940 verse, with its appeasing tendencies, but special regard to the unafraid voice of many previous poems.

In chapter 1 the focus is on the verse of Eliot and Williams, set side by side and shown creating some of their first major work by spoken address to an imaginary audience. In exuberance or defiance, the "personages" of their early poems are presented as the means by which they reach beyond the narrow self toward a wider world. But then I adjust the perspective in chapter 2 by discussing Moore's own early poems in the 1915–1918 period. For after my previous emphasis on verse-acoustics, Moore's creating of a tension between the shape of the page-text and the spoken word, whether in short rhyming stanzas or larger, more idiosyncratic configurations, adds a necessarily new dimension to the argument. It now brings to the fore the vocal-visual interplay in Williams's poetry: the contrapuntal need to regulate and channel more exactly the spoken vigor which threatens to immerse him in the world's sensuous solidity. The pull-back from such sinking—the discipline to which Moore's example encourages him—makes one especially conscious, I argue, of the way that he controls pace and line-by-line disclosure in verse that leads to his first poem in *Spring and All*.

There, as he depicts the emergence of spring and the voice from a dead-seeming landscape, Williams takes us to the conditions shared by his fellow-native in *The Waste Land*. As chapter 3 now shows, in its discussion of the poem, this is the compatriot rather than the aloof cosmopolitan who is also struggling, line by line, from beneath the soil of the unsaid and the muted. But if, by the voice's measured advance, Williams's poetic striving out of burial pinpoints a parallel in Eliot, the latter, gradually finding a way out from under silence's stultification, speech's dismemberment, and banality's noise, shows how much further than Williams he must sink into the inchoate so that he may genuinely rise. However, because Eliot earns speech's power of ascent by a kind of submergence that is more harrowing than Williams ever experienced, the poet of *The Waste Land* provides in turn a heightened awareness, as chapter 4 now suggests, of the other man's comparable but more loving impulse in *Spring and All*: Williams's urge to engage with and embrace solidities, yet keep artistically apart. So he goes down inside the colors, scents, body, and seductive appeal of the multifarious, while holding back and breaking free of potential smothering: a fall-rise pattern that at the chapter's end is shown to have its large-scale demonstration in *Paterson*—the jump into the Passaic flood countered by the upward vaulting of clarified speech.

Such acoustics have a significant animal connection that returns us, in chapter 5, to the poetry of Moore. Where previously her example brought a sound-sight tension into focus with special relevance to Williams, her poetry of the 1920s and 1930s, with its particularly wide feeling for animals, lets discussion encompass the sound of its many manifestations in the three poets' work. I describe, for instance, differing levels of intensity, but also shared impulses, behind the men-beasts enunciated by Eliot in "Sweeney among the Nightingales" and "Mr. Apollinax," as well as in the composite creature of Williams's "It Is a Living Coral," and the great animality of Moore's ice-mountain in "An Octopus." At the same time, the animal sense enlivens judgment. The noise of a Williams monster in "The Sea-Elephant" keeps one awake, I believe, to speech which stays poetically untamed in Moore, while she in turn, with the roar of an avalanche down her octopus-mountain, lets one treat the more gigantic ambitions of Williams in *Paterson* with the right degree of skepticism. Her 1932 poem "The Steeple-Jack," where sensibility finds a way home to habitable, native ground, acts also as a contrast to the very different note of exile heard in the verse of Eliot during the interwar years and after, which chapter 6 examines. Here, I suggest, the animal feeling notably changes, as Eliot's regard for body, substance, and ground becomes perilously insecure. What now becomes evident is a yearning for the auditorily "primitive" and mechanistic, together with the fatalistic, subversive beat that reverberates in *Four Quartets*.

But again a contrasting illumination is provided by Moore's poetry and her valuable animal perspective. Now her 1935 poem "Virginia Britannia," with its mockingbird cry, signals a capacity to enter native terrain lost to the later Eliot. At this point, in fact, the speaking voices of a common ground have become two not three, as the final chapter leaves discussion of Eliot behind, turning instead to the persistent vocal stamina, or otherwise, of Williams in particular, and Moore, in greater brevity, during the 1940–1962 period. Williams's 1943 "A Sort of a Song" acts here as a standard of an articulate power kept safe amidst illness, sidetracking, and the three-ply divagations of the 1950s. Yet it is also a capacity for renewal which brings us back from Williams to Eliot and Moore, as the book approaches its conclusion on a foreign shore in Williams's 1962 *Pictures from Brueghel*. Before that, however, it begins with native fact in the lots and backstreets of a distinctly American place.

Quick, Said the Bird

One

Voices of a Common Ground

For a Harvard undergraduate of 1909, a world outside the self waits to be voiced:

> This charm of vacant lots!
> The helpless fields that lie
> Sinister, sterile and blind—
> Entreat the eye and rack the mind,
> Demand your pity.
> With ashes and tins in piles
> Shattered bricks and tiles
> And the débris of a city. (IMH, 15)

"This *charm* of vacant lots!" says Eliot in "Second Caprice in North Cambridge," emphasizing the force of its spell, not its charmingness. For with assonantal stealth, the "vacant lots" of this native yet alien scene have the power, as they "lie . . . sterile and blind," to "Entreat the *eye* and rack the mind"—a torment to the "*mind*" instantly pressed further as they "De*mand* your pity." Nevertheless, such semi-spoken insistence is tranquilized by a rhyming calm (piles/tiles) as the insurgency becomes a balanced heap of

> ashes and tins
> Shattered bricks and tiles

For a New Jersey doctor of 1915, on the other hand—not set apart from his physical surroundings, but from others' tame assumptions about poetic beauty—the broken bits of an urban scene excite the voice to more constructive delight. Walking backstreets in "Pastoral," Williams lights upon the materials by which people build a sense of locality and by which he builds as a speaker. Unrhymingly, in short-line bursts of breath, he puts together

> roof out of line with sides
> the yards cluttered
> with old chicken wire, ashes,
> furniture gone wrong;
> the fences and outhouses
> built of barrel-staves
> and parts of boxes . . . (CWP1, 64)

Askewness rules, but the ear keeps order as "yards cluttered" bounce off
"sides," while the haphazard bulk of "old chicken wire" and "furniture gone
wrong" is kept in the balance by "ashes." So also the word-blocks without metrical symmetry, and without Eliot-like pacification of bricks and tiles, are ap-
preciatively weighed in the scales:

> the fences   and   outhouses
>   built of
>   barrel-staves   and   parts of boxes

Similarly poised, the "I" who continues the unfinished thrust of the sentence
(finding, "if I am fortunate," a cool, outrageous pleasure in the houses' smear
of bluish green paint) concludes by flouting expectation in another way. The
eye which momentarily thinks it is reading a modest aside in the poem's last
segment—

> No one
> will believe this

—has the assumption dashed by the final line. For this homemade place is,
audaciously,

> of vast import to the nation.

—the unhalted voice of the sentence burgeoning forth in that "import" and
springing its defiance on unbelievers.

But Williams only seems to have poetically planted himself in native
ground through pure audacity: an imaginary home constructed through a
brazen speech-style. For Eliot, however, in certain early poems, there can be
no such adoption of a vocal confidence to overcome a sense of dislocation.
Bound by the condition he described as a "fatal American introspectiveness,"[1]
he experiences the horror of being forced back upon the self in emotional inadequacy by the very *noise* of others' implorings—as if the acoustic creep of
"helpless fields" demanding your pity in "Second Caprice" is also there in the
"fatalistic horns" and "passionate violins" of "love torturing itself" in *Tristan
und Isolde* ("Opera," IMH 17, 1910), the puppet woman of "Convictions" (IMH
11, 1910) crying, "Where shall I ever find the man! / One who appreciates my
soul," and the oppressive poignancy of the older woman in the same year's
"Portrait of a Lady," seeking a soulmate in her young protégé: "The voice returns like the insistent out of tune / Of a broken violin on an August after-
noon" (CPP, 18).

But while the cacophony and the screech of passionate romanticism drive
Eliot toward the creation of a resistant persona—a character "by sound," indeed, according to the etymology—Williams discards his romantic inheritance (a sloughable Keatsian style, not an emotional threat) and creates a po-

etic "I," able to address a larger audience yet be spryly disengaged. What Eliot finds lacking in Edgar Lee Masters's verse ("a personage . . . detached from himself in order to give his meditative irony its opportunity")[2] is supplied by Williams once he has abandoned his repertoire of salutations to poetic phantoms in the early poems ("Lady of duskwood fastnesses," "Mother of flames," Apollo, Dawn, or Nature), together with the general effusion ("Waken! O people to the boughs green within you!") by which he greets his fellows in *The Wanderer* (1914) after he has taken wing with his grandmotherly muse. More specifically, the wanderer must come down in style of speech, closer to the ground and to fellow citizens of his hometown Rutherford. There, in "Tract" (1916), he can take on the manner or "personage" of an exuberant, chastising instructor:

> I will teach you my townspeople
> > how to perform a funeral—
> > for you have it over a troop
> > of artists—
> > unless you should scour the world—
> > you have the ground sense necessary.

Filling "town-", "scour," and "ground" with the full breath of airy outwardness, the eccentric tutor sweeps away all parochialism, before the expansive sentence turns back to barbed praise of those who only "have"—such pedestrians!—"the ground sense necessary." But the descent to earth keeps the voice of agility. For when Williams goes on to consider a new "design for a hearse"—a wheelless "dray to drag over the ground" in the deposing of pomp—the "*drag*" on that "*dray*" is only the prelude to the zest of release:

> Knock the glass out!
> My God!—glass, my townspeople!
> For what purpose? Is it for the dead
> to look out or for us to see
> how well he is housed or to see
> the flowers or the lack of them—
> or what?
> To keep the rain and snow from him?

The cries of mock-outrage—together with the sound of alternatives hanging in the wide-vowelled air ("to look *out* . . . to see / h*o*w well he is h*o*used . . . to see / the fl*o*wers . . .")—keep statement constantly uplifted. Though grounding a funeral in the unpretentious ("Bring him down . . . Bring him down!" as the coach-driver is told), "Tract" keeps in play an airy upwardness by question after question: "do you think you can shut grief in? / What— from us?" (the stressed "*us*" of a more generous community to which Williams finally admits his townspeople). For after his earlier *Others* version of the poem,[3] when he had over-fastened the Rutherfordians to that "one" land where "your two feet / are sucked down / so hard on it that / you cannot raise them," he thought it better to cancel the lines and end instead with the buoyancy of a larger fellowship before the townspeople are sent on their way. "Share with us / share with us," he insists, with his expansively reiterated "sh-a-re" offering a friendly taunt to the bourgeois niggards: "it will be money in your pockets."

The chastising manner can be carried further. What Ihde calls "a return to ... embodied meaning in sound,"[4] as distinct from philosophy's over-visual disembodiments, is for Williams, with gusto, the "lifting to the imagination" of "those things which lie under the direct scrutiny of the senses, close to the nose."[5] Thus he delivers a mock-rebuke to an errant organ in "Smell!": "O strong-ridged and deeply hollowed / nose of mine! what will you not be smelling?" (CWP1, 92). Taking a large breath with those stretched-out *o*'s ("O . . . holl*o*wed / n*o*se") and rising to a climax on "mine!" he can then march down the rest of the sentence with rhymed-out inevitability: "wh*a*t will you n*o*t be smelling?" With such a large rise and fall, he has shaped the spacious acoustic and its "What . . . ?" pattern which now resound in structured exuberance:

> What tactless asses we are, you and I, bony nose,
> always indiscriminate, always unashamed,
> and now it is the souring flowers of the bedraggled
> poplars: a festering pulp on the wet earth
> beneath them. With what deep thirst
> we quicken our desires
> to that rank odor of a passing springtime!

Enjoying the earthily sensuous without being submerged, he can press the attack with more questions—

> Can you not be decent? Can you not reserve your ardors
> for something less unlovely ? What girl will care
> for us, do you think, if you continue in these ways?

—but with the feigned indignance that keeps the voice tonally in the air, just above the rank-smelling ground. "Must you taste everything?" he insists; "Must you know everything? / Must you have a part in everything?": all building to the exhilarated high point where it is his poetry, not just the promiscuous nose, which has an abundant "part in EVERYthing!"

Such controlled castigation could be lauded by a later Eliot—at least in other writers. As an essayist, he celebrates Ben Jonson's rhetorical grip in the tirade by Sylla's Ghost in *Catiline*, just as he enjoys the comic severity and the detachment from romantic subjectivity of Rostand's Cyrano de Bergerac teaching a vicomte how to insult a nose.[6] But that is the ability to take the vocal initiative which he has yet to earn as the young poet of 1909–1911. As the victim of others' noisy emotionalism, he is still the tormented "I" who, in "Portrait of a Lady," must suffer the Lady's constant impingements on his inadequate personality. She is not to be fended off by the imitation-Laforgue coolness which elsewhere in the poems shrugs off over-intensity with the tones of studied cynicism, indifference, or boredom, for her voice, like an exquisite-turned-savage music, completely overwhelms. "Inside my brain a dull tom-tom begins," as the brain's beat and the metrical pound together in mechanistic iambs:

Ĭnside—mў brăin—ă dúll—tŏm-tóm—b̆egíns

As foretaste of how Eliot's auditory imagination could later rigidify into the cliché-African beat of *Sweeney Agonistes*, it is the hideous, absurd "hammering" that thrusts the speaker into distraction and a four-stress line: "Let us take the air in a tobacco trance . . ." Stretched to the limits of his unsure identity in the poem's last part and tented to the quick by the Lady, he must "borrow every changing shape / To find expression," desperately reaching beyond his human inadequacy in animal-like frenzy: "dance, dance" (or "dance, DANCE," as the repetition builds) "Like a dancing bear / Cry like a parrot, chatter like an ape": a movement, nevertheless, toward a bodied vigor and larger identity, however chained and semi-ludicrous.

For though the escapist cue is once more needed—"Let us take the air in a tobacco trance"—the "Let us" points the way to Eliot's progress as a vocalist the same year. As if in rebound from the protégé's oppression and hysteria, he issues a confident-seeming invitation to "you and I," who must hear—"go" with—the direct human talk (so it appears) and the significant animal forays of J. Alfred Prufrock's unsung "Love Song":

Let us go then, you and I,
When the evening is spread out against the sky
Like a patient etherised upon a table;
Let us go . . . (CPP, 13)

Now Eliot shares the thrill he later observes in Jonson and Donne: the potential spoken overflow, riskily pushing against boundaries, yet held back inside a vocal "outline."[7] What the Prufrock "personage" irrepressibly allows, as he moves through Boston streets, salons, and beyond, is room to sail from sky-high breeziness to prostration; from a spread-out "*evening*" to the flatly "*etherised*." Up he vaults toward a spacious future; down he comes, impelled through sordid streets of memory where half-spoken, unappeased desires echo in the sub-speech drone of "*muttering* retreats," while those "*retreats*" acoustically bring him to "*restless* nights," as "*restless*" does to "*restau*rants" with "*oyster*-shells."[8] A further "Let us go" resumes the pattern, as outgoing energy accepts instant rhyming emasculation in the room where "women come and go / Talking of Michelangelo," while a purported outstretch of truthful confession about those "narrow streets" of desire (with "lonely men in shirt-sleeves, leaning out of windows") is retracted to a frightened animal's clutch in "a pair of ragged claws."

But these are more than ironic abasements for the body. Prufrock's irrepressibility as speaker—unlike the Williams of "Tract!" and "Smell," a guise of perpetual self-exoneration more consciously taken over by Eliot from Browning's charlatans, Bishop Blougram or Sludge the medium—brings to the poem a rhythm of resilient yearning, where the voice pushes against limits, sinks back, yet in that failure has extended the boundary of the sayable. Indeed, when the "ragged claws" rhymingly scuttle across "the floors of silent seas," and those seas melt into salon enervations, where time, "Stretched on the floor, here beside you and me," is a slumbering beast, Prufrock has a firm floor of incipient animality to support his further ascents. Offering himself as Lazarus risen from the dead "to tell you all," he is not entirely dragged down to mere banality when thought of what a bored salon lady "Should say" makes him abandon the posture. For now his desire to "tell" has a more fervent basis: the instigation to stretch forth in vocal vigor rather than languor, that comes with a strong echo of Whitmanian expansiveness and persistence.

In "Vocalism"[9] Whitman is undeterred by the immensities he must work through to reach a goal of utterance "after many years":

> After treading ground, and breasting river and lake,
> After a loosen'd throat, after absorbing eras, temperaments, races, after
>   knowledge, freedom, crimes,
>   [. . .]
> After these and more, it is just possible there comes to a man, a woman, the
>   divine power to speak words. (*Leaves of Grass*, 297)

Prufrock, amidst the trivia and idleness of his days, sets the heroic music to a different key. Is serious speech "worthwhile," he asks,

> After the sunsets and the dooryards and the sprinkled streets,
> After the novels, after the teacups, after the skirts that trail along the floor—
> And this, and so much more?—
> It is impossible to say just what I mean!

Yet that bursting-out in frustration makes the lines more than a parody. Eliot has so weighed down Prufrock with the "After . . . After" burden that the resistance to sloth (as the pull-down on "floor" has its rhyme strained against by the rising note of "so much *more*?") becomes a parallel, in miniature determination, to Whitman's lengthier push across verbal barriers. Prufrock's beating iambic need "to say—just what—I MEAN!" has the energy which can—two steps forward, one step back—submit to the irritated female voice ("That is not what I meant, at all") and then go on to insist: "No! I am not Prince Hamlet, nor was meant to be." For with such firm self-limitation, he edges nearer under cover to the next comic (yet top) role available, as the Polonius-like adviser, "Full of high sentence, but a bit obtuse," and is soon presenting his credentials for the better comic-tragic part of Lear's Fool. The self-promotion becomes smilingly obvious, but while Eliot lets the reader patronize Prufrock in his aged worry about parting the hair behind or daring to eat a peach, the voice has made the most audacious extension of its boundaries since the start of the poem. "Let us go then, you and I" was the grand, sociable pretense of being at home in this America; but now, after the demeanings of rooms and streets,

> I shall wear white flannel trousers, and walk upon the beach.
> I have heard the mermaids singing, each to each.

From shore to sea—that openness where the enlarged self might genuinely have a place—Prufrock's broad lineal stride in "walk upon the beach" carries him toward the tighter, rhyming intimacy of "each to each." Despite the glum pull-back ("I do not think that they will sing to me") he has the spur for the imagination's next advance—to what, more intently, he has "seen . . . seawards":

> I have seen them riding seawards on the waves
> Combing the white hair of the waves blown back
> When the wind blows the water white and black.

The clash and clench of word on word has its exhilaration. Whatever the aged Prufrockian fancy of "white hair" combed by salon ladies-turned-mermaids, the line's youthful thrust demands that the hair "blown back," in hard, alliterative spondee, should sound like a tight mesh that word-gusts and vowels furrow open ("When . . . wind blows . . . water white") amid a zestful order. In keeping with the pattern throughout, there is a last retrenchment after so much riding on the waves:

> We have lingered in the chambers of the sea
> By sea-girls wreathed with seaweed red and brown
>   Till human voices wake us, and we drown.

No more vigorous "Combing" of hair and words will now occur in the heavy-laden repetitions of "sea-girls wreathed with seaweed." Fate entangles mortals and the tongue of pronunciation in "wreathed," "weeds," and "red;" but these Tennysonian sea-chambers, like the submarine floors scuttled across by "a pair of ragged claws," are the basis for a further upspring, this time beyond the poem. For here, clutching at contact, Prufrock has metamorphosed with consequence. Attemptedly human in faltering frankness or animal in inarticulate, sensual outreach, his voice has widened on the flood with greater possibilities for Eliot's verse. For though at the end the speaker hovers in the limbo of the not-yet-alive (and ready to die if he were), his condition points past himself to the voyagings of acoustic verse and the many voices of *The Waste Land*. There, in another transformation, one may live past the "death" of the fearful self, or fall in order to rise on the upsurge of a deeper pulse—and fate—altogether.

Reading "Prufrock" in 1918, however, Williams was more alive to the figure's limits than to Eliot's stretching of boundaries. Whatever he could find to praise ("a masterly portrait of the man just below the summit") was seriously tempered by his view of Eliot as "a subtle conformist." At the same time, his reading of comments by an Englishman, Edgar Jepson, that the poem is "securely rooted in [Eliot's] native soil" and that Prufrock is "a New World type" provoked his counter-cry that "The New World is Montezuma" (or the latter's defiant successor):[10] all before he described the Aztec ruler of Tenochtitlan in *In the American Grain* as one "so delicate, so prismatically colorful, so full of tinkling sounds and rhythms . . ."[11]

Yet if we consider auditorily what Williams by now has achieved as a poet, those "tinkling sounds" belong as much to unattainable romance as does the song of the mermaids for Prufrock. Indeed, what really matters to him are the sounds and voices of his contemporary native ground: a sense of locality to be won back from displacement with as much zeal as Eliot's creation of a multi-voiced art—American in a voyaging rather than alienated way—from his dispossessed state. For while Eliot describes himself as "an American who wasn't an American, because he was born in the South and went to school in New England . . . but wasn't a southerner in the South because his people were northerners" and "who so was never anything anywhere and who therefore felt himself to be more a Frenchman than an American and more an Englishman than a Frenchman,"[12] Williams, despite his greater positiveness ("more southern than the Southerners, and . . . as northern as if I had come from Maine")[13] must suffer Pound's jibe ("What the hell do you a bloomin' foreigner know about the place? . . . you, an effete Easterner, as a REAL American?")[14] and acknowledge the unsettling, if fruitful, contrasts of his inheritance—son of an English father, the non-American citizen distant from Williams, and of a mother with her Puerto Rican background, unfulfilled dreams of an artistic life in Paris, and despondencies. To come at the solidity of American ground as a native speaker is therefore to keep overcoming the perpetual sense of being an outsider. It is to earn naturalization or to be like the prince in Williams's destroyed early poem who wakes up in a foreign country whose "barbarous" language he cannot understand, and who must seek a way back to "a home that was his own."[15]

Finding a way home, through sea-changes and landfalls, is, in fact, the special task of his "Dedication for a Plot of Ground" (c. 1917). Here he is disciplined by the story of his father's English mother who originally conveyed him by airy magic from Paterson to the Passaic in *The Wanderer*, but whose voyages and adversities now bring him eventually toward a land dominated by a *genius loci*. Beginning respectfully—

> This plot of ground
> facing the waters of this inlet
> is dedicated to the living presence of
> Emily Dickinson Wellcome (CWP1, 105)

—the dedicator unrushedly sets out the full name in a three-beat line that is heard so frequently henceforth. So the ear is taught from the beginning to accept the longer and shorter events in the life of one

> who was born in England; married;
> lost her husband and with
> her five year old son
> sailed for New York in a two-master

and then, with the sentence prolonged to absorb more difficulty, was "driven to the Azores" before she "went" with her second husband to Puerto Rico, "bore three more children," "lost" them, and then lived a "hard" life for "eight years in St. Thomas, / Puerto Rico, San Domingo." But now, in the still-unfinished sentence, a growing impetus turns the events, so far endured without question, into a further, unbroken sequence where a woman fights to repossess what life keeps taking away, as she followed

> the oldest son to New York,
> lost her daughter, lost her "baby,"
> seized the two boys of
> the oldest son by the second marriage
> mothered them—they being
> motherless—fought for them
> against the other grandmother
> and the aunts . . .

No balk to the will is to be tolerated by a mad obstinacy that seizes the boys (their lost mother being parenthetically dashed aside). Moreover, it is "here," in her last refuge, that Emily defines, furiously and eccentrically, a distinct center—the bounds of a place beaten out in repetition, as "summer after summer" she

defended
herself here against thieves
storm, sun, fire,
against flies, against girls
that came smelling about, against
drought, against weeds . . .

Against, against, against! Rattled off by Williams in his 1945 recording[16] (but a cumulative force that *our* voicing can infer from the text's impetus) her list of enemies, real and imaginary, sounds increasingly like a multitude her agedness cannot hold back. For "against" her own weak hands and the boys' "growing strength," her resistance—"against trespassers / against rents," then finally "against her own mind"—can go no further. The thirty-seven-line sentence comes to a halt, but only so that Williams (and the speaking reader) can regain breath. With amassed authority it can be said, in a new brief paragraph:

She grubbed this earth with her own hands,
domineered over this grassy plot,
blackguarded her oldest son
into buying it, lived here fifteen years,
attained a final loneliness and—

But Williams breaks off from any hint of elegy in "final loneliness," just as he un-sticks himself, as in "Tract," from the mere earthiness of solid ground. Through the tyrannical impetus of verbs from "grubbed" to "attained" he arrives not just in a ground of solidity, where any "carcass" may come, but at its presiding spirit. Narratively standing with Emily in "this earth . . . this grassy plot . . . it . . . here," he ends the poem with a fresh two-line paragraph and a measured blast:

If you can bring nothing to this place
but your carcass, keep out.

At that moment one can hear Williams taking on the shotgun tone of his outrageous subject who, in her independent sureness, has the quality lacked by his mother, Raquel Hélène. The latter would then no longer be like the person addressed in another poem of the period, "Divertimiento" ("Miserable little woman . . . quit whining!") as he suggests a skip in the air over Main Street, "flicking the dull roof-line / with our toe-tips!," but the woman who, despite despondency, kept "true life, undefeated, if embittered."[17] Such a figure, however, could more easily be given voice by another immigrant to American ground who has similarities to the indomitable Emily. This is the Polish woman who first appears in *The Comic Life of Elia Brobitza*, the play Williams eventually published in *Others* (April/May 1919). The setting initially shares the mixture of poignancy and ashcan realism to be found in the bar scene of Edward Sheldon's 1908 play *Salvation Nell*[18] (an influential model in his early days for Williams's fellow-member of the Provincetown Players, Eugene O'Neill), especially when Brobitza starts the drama as a "solitary girl" in the street, vainly trying to entice home her drunken husband, Jim. Knocked down by him, she nevertheless laughs "and laughs again, harder and harder to herself": an indication of the un-poignant, reckless humor that continues as the scene changes to a room "with soiled and torn wallpaper" in an empty house. There she has become an old woman getting into bed, but having the bravado to convince the Poor Master and another officer of the parish, on their arrival, that, though partly undressed, she is naked and cannot be evicted:

> *She.* There's my things drying in the corner;
> that blue skirt joined to the grey shirt.
> I'm sick of trouble.
> Lift the covers if you want me
> and you'll see the rest of my clothes—
> though it would be cold laying with nothing on!
>
> *P.M. (Looks sharply at the other who is laughing)*
> What's so funny, huh?
>
> *She.* I won't work and I got no cash;
> what are you going to do about
> it?—and no jewelry—the crazy
> fools! But I've my two eyes and a
> smooth face and here's this, look!
> it's high! there's brains and blood in there!
> My name's Brobitza!
> *(Pause. She looks up slyly as the officer makes as if to draw back the covers)*
> Corsets can go to the devil and
> drawers along with them! What do I care.
> *(She laughs coarsely. The man is convulsed.)*
>
> *P.M. (Disgusted)*
> You ain't got no clothes on?
> Well, damn your soul. You old she-devil!

After the two men leave, romantic fantasy takes over. Brobitza becomes young again, woken in the light of "florescent green" by Flavi, her peasant lover, with gifts and new clothes. At the stroke of midnight, she is turned back into an old woman, but one who dies laughing as the parish officers carry her out.

But all this, together with the play format, obstructs Williams's ultimate intentions. For him it is more vital when making a poem from the play and not the other way round (as now becomes evident, despite the play's 1919 publication date)[19] to extract a singular voice from drama's hampering. Cut clear of stage directions, scene changes, pathos, and fantasy, Brobitza (renamed as the youthful Robitza in "Portrait of a Woman in Bed") can now speak without being interrupted by the now-silent officers. The poem's short-line form also reveals what the play's layout hid: the vocal pattern of defiant, staccato outbursts that potentially could break into disconnected pieces but which, against gravity, are held together by Robitza's ever-eruptive force:

> There's my things
> drying in the corner;
> that blue skirt
> joined to the grey shirt—
>
> I'm sick of trouble!
> Lift the covers
> if you want me
> and you'll see
> the rest of my clothes—
> though it would be cold
> lying with nothing on!
>
> I won't work
> and I've got no cash.
> What are you going to do
> about it?
> —and no jewelry
> (the crazy fools)
>
> But I've my two eyes
> and a smooth face
> and here's this! look!
> it's high!
>
> There's brains and blood
> in there—
> My name's Robitza!
> Corsets
> can go to the devil—
> and drawers along with them—
> What do I care! (CWP1, 87)

"What do *I* care!" The emphatic independence is as clear as the insistence on "*my* things" implied at the start, together with all the splenetic thrusts, defined by line-breaks ("sick of trouble!"; "won't work"; "got no cash"; "and no jewelry") which, after a snapped aside ("the crazy fools") lets her leap across the stanza-gap to a new thought and initiative: "But I've my two eyes." With that, unlike the play, she is not using a sly means to escape eviction, but (no longer having to pause now while the officer responds) can be audaciously open about her "brains and blood." Those *b*'s no longer risk entanglement with "*Brobitza*," now that "Rob*itza*," unslowed by a stage-direction, drives on to make a blunter connection with "Cor*sets*." Set on its own to hit the text-reading eye, the word belongs to the unslackened energy, crossing the line-halt ("Corsets / can go to the devil") that keeps the voice in pugnacious suspense—inside the bed and situation, yet, with uncorseted defiance, equally set apart. No longer bound by the play, where she had to respond to the Poor Master saying, "You ought to be kept in jail," she keeps a final, detached poise:

> You could have closed the door
> when you came in;
> do it when you go out.
> I'm tired.

Thus, Robitza dispatches her adversaries and retains a balance as she matches "when you came in" by the barbed suggestion of "when you go out," then letting her voice die away with "I'm t-i-red."

Tirelessly, though, the "Portrait" continues Williams's predilection for a vocally dissident poetry rooted in earthbound fact but unsaggingly tensed in independence from the ground. He works therefore toward the lift of a design where he can feel the pull of the earth, while staying in the air and not falling into the cloddishly over-literal, as he manages by the use of two opposing speakers in the 1920 "Portrait of a Lady." Unlike Eliot's poem of the same name, where voices exist in isolation, this is a dialogue of opponents clashing over the language used to describe a young lady on a swing. She herself comes directly from Jean-Honoré Fragonard's painting *La Balançoire*, where she is eyed in mid-swing by a sexually enticed young man down below—the figure remembered by Eliot in "Mr. Apollinax" (1915) as "Priapus in the shrubbery / Gaping at the lady in the swing" (CPP, 31), but characterized by Williams's poem as a speaker of particular verbosity who tells the lady: "Your thighs are appletrees / whose blossoms touch the sky" (CWP1, 129). Against such a style comes the voice of a skeptic who demands to know, more literally, "Which sky?" The lady's glorifier is forced to come down in description, dropping "below / the knees," yet not completely to earth and plain language when he says: "the tall grass of your ankles / flickers upon the shore." But this provokes another question, then another answer, and a final exchange:

> Which shore?
> the sand clings to my lips—

Which shore?—
Agh, petals may be. How
should I know?
Which shore? Which shore?
I said petals from an appletree.

The quick to-and-fro is akin to a play's dialogue, as Williams's 1950 recording usefully suggests.[20] He may have removed stage directions from the Robitza poem, but one could aptly insert some here to suggest the nuances at work:

Question: Which shore?
Answer (Harassed): The sand clings to my lips.
Question (Relentless): Which shore?
Answer (Shedding the "sand" image, but grasping at an image of other
    particles): Agh, petals may be. How should I know?
Question (More demanding): Which shore? Which shore?
Answer (Completely exasperated): I said PETALS from an appletree!

Goaded to defiance, the answerer will not be brought down to earth and sexual plainness entirely. The petals may sound like fig leaves, but, after the sand clinging to his lips, they are more like the fragmented parts and pluralities that Williams's art must instinctively hold on to and utter. They are the essential pieces derived from the sensuous mass and which, escaping the solely representational, go to make a new, sprightlier whole.

It is the plant of the composition, based on fact yet abstractly elicited from it, that Williams excitedly traces out of the church steeple in "To a Solitary Disciple" (1916). The tutoring speaker of "Tract" may here only have one pupil to address, but

See how the converging lines
of the hexagonal spire
escape upward—
receding, dividing!
—sepals
that guard and contain
the flower! (CWP1, 104)

One thinks ahead to the "centripetal" logic of the leaves in "The Crimson Cyclamen" (1936) when "the source / that has splayed out / fanwise . . . returns / upon itself in the design." Like a parallel to the increasingly bold Eliot of "Gerontion" and *The Waste Land*, who bulges a verse-sequence with upsets yet centripetally confirms a new order, Williams's outstretch and return (or engrossment in the world's phenomena countered by detachment's design) is especially audible and visible in "Great Mullen" (1920). Here separate voices, pushing against the line-curbs, and straining away from their common source or stem, antagonistically affirm a shared entirety. Two speakers pitted against each other—wifely accuser versus cool, adulterous husband—therefore hold together one tense plant-composition within the bounds of a small textual block. Only dashes separate his replies from her protests as she cries, "Liar, liar, liar!" and says of her rival:

> She is
> squirting on us both. She has had her
> hand on you!—well?—She has defiled
> ME. —Your leaves are dull, thick
> and hairy (CWP1, 162)

—as he says in the last sentence, provoking her to further rage inside the shared constriction of the form:

> Every hair on my body will
> hold you off from me. You are a
> dungcake, birdlime on a fencerail.—
> I love you, straight, yellow
> finger of God pointing to—her!

—the last word hers, as she completes and indignantly corrects his declaration of fidelity. That "her," like her final "Ha!" of scorn, defines the common boundary hemming them in.

But, as in another 1920 poem, "It Is a Small Plant," the composition can also keep its tautness by means of a single voice rather than two. Urging the sentence on past line-breaks, but with those breaks sharpening the distinctiveness of the individual units revealed, Williams continually re-knits the intrications of

> a small plant
> delicately branched and
> tapering conically
> to a point, each branch
> and the peak a wire for
> green pods, blind lanterns
> starting upward from
> the stalk each way to
> a pair of prickly edged blue
> flowerets (CWP1, 125)

Stepping with enunciatory care ("*plant* . . . *branched* . . . *tapering* . . . to a *point*") the voice, allied to the text's discipline, has the means to make "each *branch*" and "*peak*"

> a wire for
> green *pods*

where the verse-line is anchored back after the wire's branching-out. In further stretch, however,

> blind lanterns
> starting upward

light the way by the plosive effort of scaling the emphatically distinct "*p*air of *p*rickly edged *b*lue / flowerets."

Arriving at the point where a plant's "prickly" minutiae are "guarding its secret," Williams has also come close to the kind of detail which particularly engages the poetry of Moore. It is she, with her eye and ear for meticulously armored surfaces, who cuttingly tells the woman in the 1917 poem "Roses Only" that "your thorns are the best part of you," because they are "Guarding the / infinitesimal pieces of your mind" (OB, 41). At the same time, though, her dislike of social armor as an overweening defensiveness arises from her own need to create a shield and constriction in the look of the verse-text—to lay out on the page an architectured obduracy of form that both girdles an inner privacy and, from her early days as a poet, shapes forceful speech tensely and precisely. She may have said later in life that her verse sought to "preserve the spontaneous effect . . . of conversation,"[21] and that she wanted to sound as if she "had not thought it before and were talking to you. Unstrained and natural,"[22] but there she forgets the rigor and strenuous enunciations of her mind's youthful voice, defined by and pursuing its unbroken path through the visual impediment of syllable-counted stanzas or quirkily insistent line-breaks.

It is the creative clash between heard speech and seen form which here enters the argument: like the resistance of voice to the printed text, which Bruce R. Smith describes in *The Acoustic World of Early Modern England*,[23] but which arises from Moore's particular sense of opposites—the would-be constraints of text and social deadness pushed against by vocal insurgency—which she, of all three poets, brings to special prominence in her first important poems of 1915 to 1918. Examining these in the next chapter, I now seek to add an extra dimension to what has so far been largely discussed as voices, "personages" or "some good characters" (of which Eliot wanted more from Williams when he met him)[24] whether in the form of outgoing address, dialogue, or solitary speech, with the effect of syntax, sentences, rhyme or non-rhyme, conventional metrics, or word-block balancings. Moore's example takes us further, to the governing frame which holds such effects together; for what discussion of Williams's short-line poems has only indicated, and what is to become more explicitly important in the treatment of Eliot's later verse-paragraphs—

visual containment cramming acoustic variety inside itself to the point of spillage—is the tension which Moore makes central. If Eliot and Williams are dislocated from their native scene, and seek a way back to newly occupiable ground, Moore, another foreigner in her own country—rejecting those who would reject her style of speech—brings into play the figures and multitudes of a sounded world which now is hers alone, and no other's.

Two

To Hew Form Truly

"Picasso . . . You hew form truly."

E. E. CUMMINGS

Bluffing familiarity ("Let us go then, you and I") is one style of address. Sprightly demand is another: "You! / to go with me a-tip-toe," as Williams tells a non-existent "band" of fellows in his 1915 "Sub Terra." But Moore, with an exclamatory directness toward "You" the same year, neither dances tiptoe with an imaginary clan nor reaches out in Prufrockian fancy toward companions of the sea. Instead she mitigates her sense of cultural isolation by celebrating the larger cultural milieu where she, the unknown nobody from Carlisle, Pennsylvania, and Chatham, New Jersey, can be on speaking terms—at least in verse—with figures such as Browning, Yeats, George Moore, Shaw, and others. In particular, she addresses the "You" who stands out from the uncomprehending crowd in a poem she later called "To a Strategist" but which here, in its first publication, is "To Disraeli on Conservatism":

> You brilliant Jew,
> You bright particular chameleon, you
>   Regild a shabby fence.
>
> They understood
> Your stripes and particolored mind, who could
>   Begrudge you prominence
>
> And call you cold!
> But when has Prejudice been glad to hold
>   A lizard in its hand,
>
> Or kindred thing?
> To flesh fed on a fine imagining,
>   Sound flesh is contraband.[1]

Here restrictions in verse-form are as much a barrier to be leaped as petty concepts. Tercet symmetry (3-11-6 syllables in the first two stanzas; 4-10-6 in the second pair); the eye and ear partly detained by capital-letter line-starts or line-end rhymes: all intensifies the unstopped vehemence of a voice set going from the first lines' emphatic rhymes ("You . . . Jew, / You") to the "*brilliant*

... *bright*" enunciation of politics' (and the stage's)[2] mercurial creature, and thence to the extra-accented force of "Regild"—Disraeli outshining the front bench or "fence" of parliamentary colleagues as well as giving the lie to Paul Elmer More's remarks on his "shabby strain" of language and "cold malignant strokes."[3] Those who called Disraeli "cold!"—the word contemptuously resonating against "*could*"—have their mean power to "Be*grudge*" hit against by the judicious syllables of "Pre*judice*" ("But when has Prejudice been glad to hold . . . ?"). What it cannot hold (the sentence's onward thrust ignoring the obvious rhyme with "cold") is the Disraelian animal: the lizard who, distinct from rarefied "flesh fed on a fine imagining," is, by Moore's own chameleon shift of emphasis, "*Sound* flesh"—to be solidly grasped by a sound that, firmer than the rhyme with "hand," smuggles its value to the listener by the protrusive syllables of "*contra*band."

Eliot describes this kind of effect as "giving a word a slightly more analytical pronunciation, or stressing a syllable more than ordinarily." But there, in his introduction to Moore's *Selected Poems* (1935), he is praising her mastery of "light rhyme," when such a term seems too slight a portrayal of the anti-chiming muscularity that thrives so frequently on opposition in her verse. Enclosures are there to be pushed against from the inside, as in the thrust of another 1915 poem, "To a Man Working His Way Through the Crowd," which also celebrates a heroic individualist, Gordon Craig. This pioneer of modern stage-space (whose design for Mark Antony's scene of oratorical triumph over resistance, "The man who is persuading the crowd," would seem to prompt Moore's title)[4] claims in one preface: "I am moving towards a new theatre. . . . All that I have put in the book now lies behind me."[5] So, by the same spirit, the formal boundaries in Moore's last two stanzas (each under the discipline of 8-16-13 syllables) exist in order to be cleaved past by the discriminating voice:

> The most propulsive thing you say,
> Is that one need not know the way
>   To be arriving. That foreword smacks of retrospect.
>
> Undoubtedly you overbear,
> But one must do that to come where
>   There is a space, a fit gymnasium for action.[6]

The "say-way" tinkle of rhyme in the first two lines only enhances the undetained propulsion of the sentence toward its real, firm halt at "*arriving.*" Like "That foreword" to Craig's book, already outpaced by his vision and now smacking of "retrospect," Moore's final stanza leaves qualms behind as emphases press toward a last arrival-point. For though "Un*dou*btedly you overbear" (word bearing on word) "one must *do* that to come" (in mouth-widening room) "*where* / There is a space"—and that "sp*ace*" athletically extended as a "fit gymnasium." Extended further, Craig's stage—and Moore's poetic space also[7]—is a "gymnasium for *action*": the last word orally singled out in springy distinctness from "gymnasium."

Yet for all Moore's enactment of the vigor in her addressed heroes (as when the subject of her 1915 poem, "To Bernard Shaw: A Prize Bird," brings down opponents with "Samson's pride") her style of overthrowing the inimical or the perverse has its deliberate self-curbing. Her attack upon pseudo-grandeur and the morally inert, for example, has to be matched in sovereign boldness by a discipline that equally shuns arrogance: a zest-restraint tension as vital to the art as the text-voice interplay, and shown most notably when she sets up formal limits like a cramping mentality she can deride from inside and vocally work her way out from. So while she urges Shaw to "strut, colossal bird" in the "barnyard" of lesser talents, her way of chiding the symbol of decayed authority, the Egyptian Ibis in "To Statecraft Embalmed" (1915), has to be more clearly subversive, as she keeps within the unvoluble rules of a statecraft that clasps its empty mystique to itself and silences criticism:

> There is nothing to be said for you. Guard
> Your secret. Conceal it under your "hard
>   Plumage," necromancer.
>   O
> Bird, whose "tents" were "awnings of Egyptian
> Yarn," shall Justice' faint, zigzag inscription—
> Leaning like a dancer—
>   Show
> The pulse of its once vivid sovereignty?

The line-starts were later reduced to lowercase. But, as shown by this first printing of the poem in the December 1915 *Others*, Moore originally created for the eye, with her capitals and quotation marks, the fortress-like appearance of a "hard / Plumage," the only cracks in the monolith being the gaps made by the open vowels of "O," "Show," and their successors. Thus, whatever the hoarding of a "*secret*" by the sealing-in of "con*ceal*" (with "necromancer" also guarding the "*secret*") the wide breath of "O / Bird" breaks into the deathly huddle of sound. Shall the old, seemingly awry, yet non-despotic idea of Justice ("faint, zigzag . . . Leaning") still persist? Shall it, "Leaning like a dancer" (not collapsed, but ready for an upspring, perhaps) "Show" its former "vivid sovereignty"? The questions open out into the air, and though, very soon, "you," deadly statecraft, would shut down on vocal and political sprightliness (as when "with moribund talk / Half limping . . . you stalk / About") the stiffness of such verbal joints is to be met later by the poet's poise: "*Ibis*, we find"—concisely suiting the un-garrulous occasion—"No / Vir*tue* in you."

"You," and wartime's emotional deadening, are the target of even more

succinct remonstrance in "To the Soul of 'Progress'" (*The Egoist*, April 1915:
later entitled "To Military Progress"):

> You use your mind
> Like a millstone to grind
>   Chaff.
>
> You polish it
> And with your warped wit
>   Laugh
>
> At your torso

Spoken as an onward thrust, the poem demands that the rhymes crowd so
abruptly against each other that a millstone "mind" is heard to "gr*ind* / Chaff"
in the crush of the spondee, with "warp*ed* w*it*" more intensely polishing "*it*"
and a merciless, military "L*augh*" scattered like "Ch*aff*" as it contemplates
the sacrificed body of an army. By the same ear for verbal near-collisions in
another poem, Moore also ensures that the words of un-atrophied spontaneity
take on a new, bright edge—as when a boy's unsophisticated remark about his
father in "'He Wrote the History Book,' It Said" (the original title in *The Egoist*
of May 1916) is the means to cut through the sanctimonious:

> There! You shed a ray
>   Of whimsicality on a mask of profundity so
> Terrific, that I have been dumbfounded by
> It . . .

"*There!*" indeed Moore emphatically drives an impetus and illumination
through the opaquely grandiose, making "a ray / Of whimsical*ity*" penetrate
the mask of adult "profund*ity*" in a way so pressingly "TERRIFIC" (the adjective intensified in sound and sight at the capital-letter beginning of the
original line) that "dumb*found*ed" emerges from "pro*fund*ity" with extra
astonishment.

It is just as apt that she who breaches perverse bastions by her intimate
knowledge of defensiveness should cut through moral sham in "Pedantic Literalist" (1916). The person of doubtful good will who pedantically keeps to
the letter of the law rather than the true spirit of fellowship is addressed, in
an extraordinary opening image, as "Prince Rupert's drop"—the glassmaker's
molten blob which, cooled and made fragile by water, can be exploded at the
merest pinch of a finger. If that suggests illusory spirituality (like the further
address to the "literalist" as "paper muslin ghost, / White torch"), the drop
also has its historical connotation as the toy of Charles I's nephew, Prince Rupert of Bavaria, who introduced it to the court in the 1640s, when the King is
said to have used it to play tricks on unsuspecting victims. Against Cavalier

frivolity, however, Moore places the words of Anglican sternness (also from
the 1640s) by her own special reading of Richard Baxter's *The Saint's Everlasting Rest.* For in speaking to "you," the cruel sentimentalist, she must insist that

> "with power to say unkind
> Things with kindness, and the most
> Irritating things in the midst of love and
> Tears," you invite destruction. (OB, 33)

Where Baxter speaks of ministers who betray their flock by letting them avoid
their consciences ("How gently do we handle those sins which will handle so
cruelly our people's souls!")[8] Moore builds with intensity toward "the most /
Irritating things." So also in stanza three she transforms a noun in Baxter's
chapter title, "Reprehending the General Neglect of the Heavenly Rest,"[9] into
a tart verb, showing that the literalist

> "neglected to be
> Painful, deluding him with
> Loitering formality,"
> "Doing its duty as if it did it not,"
> Presenting an obstruction

To the motive that it served . . .

Compacting Baxter's injunctions not to "delude thyself" (by lazy thoughts
about heaven), to "take heed of [spiritual] loitering," and to abhor empty "formality" ("This doing of duty as if we did it not")[10] Moore conjoins two Baxter words ("Loitering formality") and cuts straight to the literalist's bizarre
self-contradictions.

Nor, by textual break-up and varied line-length, are such darts of precision
allowed to lose their edge when they appear in larger syllabic stanzas. The new
acuity of exactly positioned words hits the ear and eye even more profusely in
"Critics and Connoisseurs" (as it first appeared in the July 1916 *Others*) when
she again pits her delight in a child's impromptu act against crabbed hauteur.
This time, though, she matches the connoisseurship of the art snob with her
belief in "Life's faulty excellence," as she calls it in "To Statecraft Embalmed,"
and which here, in the form of "unconscious / Fastidiousness," describes a

> Mere childish attempt to make an imper-
>   fectly ballasted animal stand up.
> A determination ditto to make a pup
>   Eat his meat on the plate.

Not so "Mere" in its sardonic, capitalized appearance, this "attempt to make"

an
*an*imal
st*an*d

up, in acoustic alignment, has its partial success for the child, despite the near-wobble of the "imperfectly b*all*asted anim*al*." So too, with unwavering intent ("A *de*termination *ditto*") and in the poem's three-word pattern, an attempt to

make   a   pup
Eat   his   meat
on   the   plate

almost squares up, even though "*meat*" will not exactly rhyme with, or unspillingly stay on that "p*l*ate." But this is preferable to the initial disdaining of food by the standoffish purist or critic whom a swan resembles on the Cherwell in Oxford:

It stood out to sea like a battle-
ship. Disbelief and conscious fastidiousness were
the staple
Ingredients in its
Disinclination to move. Finally its hardi-
hood was not proof against its
Inclination to detain and appraise such bits
Of food as the stream

Bore counter to it; it made away with what I gave it
To eat . . .

Though "*Dis*belief," "fasti*di*ousness," and "Ingre*di*ents" sound out a stubbornness, the unbudged *in*sistencies of the "*In*gredients *in* its / Dis*in*clination to move" can bend sufficiently to let the lordly swan "detain and appraise" (with no loss of dignity in its new "*In*clination") what it must cross the stream and stanza-gap to seize. Like the bird with the "b*it*s / Of food," word tightens on word as "*it* made away with what I gave *it* / To *eat*"—"it" and "eat" no more exactly rhyming than "meat" and "plate," but close enough, in more faulty excellence, to swallow those pieces all the same. Being an aloof "battleship" swan is thus no more tenable a state than that of the "fastidious ant carrying a stick" on its punctilious errands in the final stanza:

What is
There in being able
To say that one has dominated the stream
in an attitude of self-defense,

In proving that one has had the experience
Of carrying a stick?

What *is* there, indeed? The note of chiding amazement struck at the poem's conclusion is akin to that caught at another's beginning—

In This Age of Hard Trying, Nonchalance Is Good and
"Really . . .

—where ("*Really!*") Moore cannot believe (as who could, surely?) that the over-earnest think it "the / Business of the gods to bake clay pots."[11] In an Age of Hard Trying where sanity's bemusement is applied to those who would laboriously carry a Rooseveltian Big Stick, it is just as important to query the earnest-seeming aggression, the "hard majesty" of a "sophistication," in "Those Various Scalpels" (1917).[12] Despite the fierce surfaces of a woman— "your hair, the tails of two fighting-cocks . . . your . . . hand // A / Bundle of lances"—the defensive weaponry might, after all, be treated as scalpels, the finely cutting blades of discrimination, when Moore asks the sophisticate:

why
dissect destiny with instruments which
Are more highly specialized than the tissues of destiny itself?

Again one observes how the mockery of minuscule calculations by a scalpel-sharp acoustic ("why / *dissect des*tiny . . . ?") comes from Moore's own knowledge of defensiveness—the need to be armored against others' rejection of her own distinctive sensibility. But her strong animal sense, with its capacity to expand beyond the ego into a range of creaturely roles, like Eliot's energizing escape into an array of many voices, has a notable inclusiveness. As shown by the 1919 poem "In the Days of Prismatic Colour," her feeling for a "perpendicular" or upright truth equally accommodates a wide span of oblique variations, or, with centipede-like motion in these post-Adamic times, a "classic // multitude of feet." So too, more encompassingly, with an animal hide round spiritual inwardness, she can move out in a world of physical variety through the voice of an elephant in "Black Earth":

Openly, yes,
With the naturalness
Of the hippopotamus or the alligator
When it climbs out on the bank to experience the

Sun, I do these
Things which I do, which please
No one but myself.

Yet in this 1918 version of the poem[13] the "I" does not spread in vocal self-centering. With textual pull-back exerted against the voice's outer push, phrasing may bound forth with gusto ("Openly, yes") but at the smallest point of visual contraction in the stanza. Statement's exuberance lets us hear an *op*enness both sharable with the "hipp*op*otamus" and the outward-climbing alligator in the maximum stretch of the stanza's end, before the next stanza's visual contraction—offering the pleasure of the "Sun" rather than the alligator's killed prey—tightens back the self of animal outreach to an "I" of unboastful restriction. "I do these / Things which I do" (action hemmed in by repetitive verb) with a restraint that later has the quality of a "spiritual poise." For this self with "sensitized ears" is a counter to the ego's "Wandlike body of which one hears so much." Auditorily, therefore, the poet-elephant takes the measure of

> That tree-trunk without
> Roots, accustomed to shout
>   Its own thoughts to itself like a shell

and leaves behind the "*sh*out / *sh*ell" echo-chamber of "it*self*" for the different inwardness and power of "black earth":

>   That on which darts cannot strike decisively the first

> Time, a substance
> Needful as an instance
>   Of the indestructibility of matter; it
>   Has looked at the electricity and at the earth-

> Quake and is still
> Here;

Now squeezed form enacts the retreat of animality and spirit to an irreducible core. With external darts failing to "str*i*ke dec*i*sively the first // T*i*me," the /ai/ contracts to the inward /i/ of "*i*nstance": the rhyme with "substance" ignored by an "*in-*" which prefers, emphatically, to instance "the *in*destructibility of matter" (with a tiny, uncrushable "it" inside the "indestructibil*it*y"). Enduring cataclysm, "it" has calmly "looked at the electric*ity* and at the earth- // Quake" (in the quake's spondaic word-split) "and is still"—with pronounced monosyllabic firmness —"*Here.*"

Nevertheless, "Black Earth" did not remain in Moore's collected verse after 1951. Even under its later title of "Melanchthon" (and under the moral cover of the Protestant reformer Philipp Schwarzerdt, who himself overlaid his German identity by translating his name into Greek) it may well have seemed to the later poet, who by that time had ceased to be a literary outsider, far too dissident and assertive. Certainly it is more self-revealing about inward "power" and not as hidden in its disclosure of animal vitality behind a hard surface as "The Fish." One's eye, reading that poem, as here in *The Egoist* of August 1918, has no typographic encouragement from the unindented stanzas to penetrate an undersea interior:

> The Fish
> Wade through black jade.
> Of the crow-blue mussel-shells, one
> Keeps adjusting the ash-heaps;
> Opening and shutting itself like
>
> An injured fan.

Even when the voice reads the title as the first line of the poem, it has to pull against visual fixity and be halted almost immediately by the "Wade/jade" abruptness of rhyme. In its odd conjunction of the lowly and luxurious, the sentence shares for a moment the insistent, rhymed symmetry of a Hardy poem, "The Convergence of the Twain," that Moore knew from *Satires of Circumstance*.[14] On the sunken *Titanic*,

> Dim moon-eyed fishes near
> Gaze at the gilded gear
> And query: "What does this vaingloriousness down here?"
> (*The Collected Poems of Thomas Hardy*, 288)

But Moore is not detained by droll irony. When, in revised layout,

> The Fish
> Wade
> through black jade

they let more light into the opaque block. They expose the indented stanza pattern to which the poem undeviatingly adheres, but a syllabic grid that now has the look of an arbitrary rigidity which *spoken* syntax (cut to fit it in written form) defies by its unbrokenness and changes of pace. Slow wading is succeeded—and conspicuously now in the clash of speech and typography — by articulation's more determined thrust:

> Of the crow-blue mussel shells, one
>   keeps
>   adjusting the ash-heaps;
> opening and shutting itself like
>
> an
> injured fan. (OB, 43)

Uncompromising sentence-reversal ("Of the crow-blue . . .") demands the voice's extra obduracy as it picks out from "mu*ssel shells*," with unslurred distinctness, the particularity of "one" that, in the comedy of enunciation and prising apart, "keeps / *adjusting* the *ash*-heaps" where their "opening" is instantly succeeded by the adroit pronunciation of "*sh*utting it*s*elf"—the pace hastened as the to-and-fro of a briefly glimpsed inner life closes down inside the tight rhyme of "an / injured fan."

Yet an opening has been made, as the whimsically slight injury to a surface signals what might be more fully revealed by faster cuts into an undersea casing. Thus "The barnacles which encrust the / side / of the wave" in stanza two are speedily searched by the onward-driving voice as (stanzas three and four) the submerged shafts of the

> sun
> split like spun
>   glass, move themselves with spotlight swift-
>   ness
>   into the crevices—
> in and out illuminating
>
> the
> turquoise sea
>   of bodies.

Words are whittled to cut the finer: pronunciation unthickening "*sh*afts" to let "*su*bmerged" beams of the "*su*n" acoustically "*sp-l*-it" into "*sp*un glass," while the word of rapidity itself is sliced smaller to get the sun's flickering "swift- / ness / *i*nto the crev*i*ces." But, for all the kaleidoscopic delights of "the / turquoise sea" enjoyed by Moore, the submarine inwardness of her sensibility remains unplumbed. It takes a sharper penetration of externals to suggest it than she could manage in the 1918 version, where she says, with an eye to undersea refraction, "The water drives a / Wedge of iron into the edge / Of the cliff." There she seems to remember Emerson's poem, "Sea-Shore," and the voice of the "chiding Sea": "I drive my wedges home, / And carve the coastwise mountain into caves."[15] But in revision (setting "iron" against "iron" and replacing "into" with "through") she carves more deeply. Now, as

> The water drives a
>   wedge
>   of iron through the iron edge
> of the cliff

there is greater damage to outer defenses than an injury to a fan—the breakages visually mimicked by the layout in stanzas six and seven:

    All
    external
        marks of abuse are present on
            this
            defiant edifice—
    all the physical features of

    ac-
    cident—lack
        of cornice, dynamite grooves, burns
        and hatchet strokes . . .

But the blows, like the textual impingements, cut only into the outside of a reef and poetic toughness. "All / external / marks . . . all the physical features" are gathered up by the voice of inner indomitableness, clustering its power in "*defiant edifice*," and using assonantal pressure ("*edifice . . . physical*") with hard-edged rhyme ("ac- . . . lack") to impel momentum forward in a steady outlasting of superficial violence (and a mock-decorative "lack / of cornice"). External dilapidations therefore deceive. For though the undersea "chasm-side" may seem "dead," "Repeated / evidence" in the final stanza (clashing "evidence" against "*dead*") acoustically suggests the proof that it can still "live / on what cannot revive / its youth." To the last, the young poet keeps the secret of that replenishing energy; but with "*live*" set against the sound of flagging in "cannot re*vive*," a sustenance endures: "The sea grows old in it."

Safeguarding a buried life by staying inside form's rigid carapace, Moore thus projects outwards the thrusts, agilities, and surprises of a unique speaking voice. She has taught herself in these poems the lesson of pull-back as a means to leap forward, and in that she accentuates starkly what Eliot already knows in "Prufrock" as a pattern of retreat-to-advance. But the very blatancy by which visual containment in her poetry defines the vocal force cutting against it also takes us further: to a later, pre–*Waste Land* Eliot in the 1919 "Gerontion," where the verse-paragraph has become a lineal frame shaken by unappeased energies. In spondee-replete lines, varying from three-stress to six, the weary Gerontion voice swells into ferocious life, sinks back, and startlingly reemerges—an "old man in a dry month" who may deny his presence at Thermopylae's "hot gates" yet battles ever more vehemently through history's mire and a taut participle toward spat-out fricatives ("Bitten by *flies, fought*"): all before he fades away at the paragraph's end with the singsong passivity by which he began: "A dull head among windy spaces."

Before the poem's end, however, a greater antiquity blows through this small modern agedness and its paltry self-limiting. Though "a thousand small deliberations / Protract the profit of their chilled delirium" and "Excite the membrane, when the sense has cooled"—the antithetical halves of the last two lines pattering neatly in support of the verse-boundary—the voice is being excited beyond such well-balanced safety to "multiply variety," like a latter-day Epicure Mammon, "In a wilderness of mirrors," only for that to be the "*wilderness*" that lets through the "*will . . . will . . . ?*" of a genuine danger in the questions now continuing. After "Christ the tiger" and his devourings earlier in the poem, a further animality is about to be loosed upon the inhabitants of the Gerontion house:

> What will the spider do,
> Suspend its operations, will the weevil
> Delay? De Bailhache, Fresca, Mrs. Cammel, whirled
> Beyond the circuit of the shuddering Bear
> In fractured atoms. Gull against the wind in the windy straits
> Of Belle Isle, or running on the Horn. (CPP, 37)

The full force of the vocal impetus, however, is only unleashed through initial restraint. Whereas one rhetorical source, Tourneur's revenger,[16] presses home his attack ("Does the silk-worm expend her yellow labours / For thee For thee does she undo herself?") Eliot notably forces *his* "do" to hover in "Suspend . . . ?" and lingers out the menace of "Del-a-ay . . . ?"—a holding back of energy by the questioner's uprisen voice in order to lunge forward more terribly as "*Delay*" sweeps away the "thousand small *deliberations*" as well as *De* Bailhache and the others. The "will . . . will . . . ?" of possibility becomes the all-out "*whirled / Beyond*," where the nonstop momentum which changes the "fractured atoms" of the stultified into a battling bird-vision—"Gull against the wind, in the windy straits," with "*straits*" emphasized by extra wind in the lengthened line, blowing against paragraph straitness—carries us with the gull of Canada's Belle Isle to the fearless bird who is "running on the Horn" of Cape and danger. All this would be a vocal windiness, far exceeding the dormant bounds of the Gerontion mind, or Eliot's inclusive capacity, were it not that the next line—"White feathers in the snow, the Gulf claims"—claims back such flight as frozen scatterings: a halt to the onrush demanded, as the winds (now unthreatening, commercial "Trades") drive the old man "To a sleepy corner" and a small lineal nook at the paragraph's end.

But, after "Prufrock," and now even more after "Gerontion," the force of bird, sea, and wind has left its mark on Eliot's sense of the verse-frame and its possibilities. The pressure on boundaries (with the "personage" concept ballooned out to near bursting-point in the speaker's inclusion of so many historic energies, torpors, and sudden changes) is not only a forecast of the multi-vocal paragraphs yet to appear in *The Waste Land*. It also shows the essential difference between Eliot's syntax-adherent poetry—an utterable address to a listener, however bizarre, in moment-by-moment unfolding—and contemporary avant-garde experiments in sound, such as Filippo Marinetti's *parole in libertà*, the *zaum* of Russian Futurists,[17] "bruitist" noise,[18] or the *Lautegedicht* of Hugo Ball at the Dadaists' Cabaret Voltaire, where a common aim is the total disjunction of sense and syntax. Such exploding of norms, both then and later, opens the way, it is claimed, to the possibility of a new language,[19] but it is English as spoken here and now, vitalized by acoustic upsets, astonishings, or foreign tongues (as in *The Waste Land* to come) which increasingly matters to Eliot—a vindication of the verse-sequence only achievable by insurgency.

We come back, in fact, to what he shares with Moore's defensive syllabic structures, invigorated and flouted by the orality they shape. But she, as the poet of inner privacy and outward-moving determination, points us also to Williams. While she must pull against her own natural secrecy, and go forth into a heterogeneous world, he, resisting excess in his instinctive outreach to particularities—and a potential drowning in sensuous fact—must go the other way. His special regard is not for her poetic outgoings but for her restraints. What he seeks is to regulate the energy which instinctively carries him outward, for example, in "Spring Strains" (1916):

> In a tissue-thin monotone of blue-grey buds
> crowded erect with desire against
> the sky—
>
>   tense blue-grey twigs
> Slenderly anchoring them down, drawing
> them in—
>
>   two blue-grey birds chasing
> a third struggle in circles, angles,
> swift convergings to a point that
> bursts instantly! (CWP1, 97)

As twigs pull down upon an outreaching desire, word-blocks on the page are braced against each other to make a tense, compositional whole which is—as the birds "struggle in circles, angles, / swift convergings"—more highly charged than, but just as geometric as, the steeple's "dark converging lines" in the 1916 "To a Solitary Disciple": another design more important to Williams than any surrender to luscious impressions of a "shell-pink" moon or "turquoise" sky.

But he needs to go further, and it is a sign of his regulatory intent, sharpened by Moore, that in a 1921 issue of *Contact* he introduced two of her poems, "Those Various Scalpels" and "In the Days of Prismatic Colour," by saying: "In spite of a Whitman, windy-prairie tradition it is possible to rate a threshing machine lower than more delicate mechanisms, and to find that gusto,

bigness, and splurge lack force through not being able to withstand diagno-
sis."[20] Pound's teasing of Williams may here be remembered ("Would Harriet
[Monroe], with the swirl of the prairie wind in her underwear, or the virile
Sandburg recognize you, an effete Easterner, as a REAL American? . . . You
have never seen the projecting and protuberant Mts. of the Sierra Nevada.")[21]
but Williams, who implicitly answered Pound in part by *his* un-Sandburgian
assertion ("to hell with singing the States and the plains and the Sierra Ne-
vadas for their horses' vigor")[22] can best become a real American poet, with
his own version of Moore's later "delicate" yet tough "mechanisms," when he
pulls back on possible "bigness and splurge" in the large-scale action of his
"Overture to a Dance of Locomotives" (1917).

Passengers and porters on the move in a railroad station; a train about to
leave for a vast terrain: all is subject to control by the "disaccordant hands"
of the station clock, "straining out from / a center," just as, centripetally, everything that shoots off at odd angles is reined back by the timely pattern
of a musical bar, in a progressive halving: "two—twofour—twoeight!" That
remains, even as the locomotive's "dingy cylinders" strain "against the hour,"
and a whistle signals the train's departure:

Not twoeight. Not twofour. Two!

Gliding windows. Colored cooks sweating
in a small kitchen. Taillights—

In time: twofour!
In time: twoeight!

—rivers are tunneled; trestles
cross oozy swampland: wheels repeating
the same gesture remain relatively
stationary: rails forever parallel
return on themselves infinitely.
The dance is sure. (CWP1, 146)

And so it is because of Williams's insistence that one hears the upward curve
("Not twoeight. Not twofour") descending emphatically on "*Two!*": an even,
spoken beat rather than an indicator of gathering speed. Under that acoustic
order the fleeting bits of movement (windows, cooks sweating, "Taillights—")
are subjugated to the rise-fall steadiness of phrasing ("In time: twofour! /
In time: twoeight!") which governs the larger spans of action, in statement's
upsurge and descent, as "rivers are tunneled" and "trestles / cross . . ." The
rhythmic structure of action, not the representation of the locomotive's rush
through tunnels and over trestles, is the sentences' concern as the wheels' repetition, like repeated movements in the station beneath the clock, asserts the

"relatively / stationary": the point of steady suspense, beaten out for the ear, as "rails . . . return on themselves infinitely."

It is a stillness within movement to be seized without stopping the action. This is no Cubist painting like Umberto Boccioni's 1912 triptych "States of Mind" ("Stati d'animo") set in a railroad station, where a locomotive's number 6943 juts out from swirls of steam. Nor does Williams's wresting of a design from fast action in "The Great Figure" (1919) stiffen into the kind of fixed number that Charles Sheeler's 1925 painting "The Figure Five in Gold" extracts from the same poem. For even as the latter's short-line form slows the speed of a different machine, a New York fire truck from district five, Williams insists that any control of movement must be part of an unhalted vocal onwardness:

> Among the rain
> and lights
> I saw the figure 5
> in gold
> on a red
> firetruck
> moving
> tense
> unheeded
> to gong clangs
> siren howls
> and wheels rumbling
> through the dark city. (CWP1, 174)

Thus "I saw the figure *five*" (as it must be stressed, when spoken), with the sign looming out of an unfocused background where iambics urge the voice forward, but not too fast. Where lineal brevities ensure the pronounced distinctness of individual words and phrasings, there is time to pinpoint the figure as an abstraction, a higher order amidst sensuous color (like the geometric lines of "To a Solitary Disciple") just as one sees and hears the colors—

> in gold
> on a red

—cut away from the solid thing. But this is only because the sentence carries forward

> on a red
> firetruck

—momentum still letting the eye appreciate each discrete segment before, with increasing pace, the poem lets through the noise of fire truck actuality: the crash of units against one another in "*gong clangs*," with the dissonant rumble of "wh*eels*" against "siren h*owls*."

Thus, snatched from the onward movement "through the dark city," a structural brightness persists in the mind—an image of suspense amidst mobility that levitation's nimbleness maintains in a different way throughout "To Waken an Old Lady" (1920). Here, in an unstopped spoken sentence,

> Old age is

—with surprise, after the line-break—

> a flight of small
> cheeping birds
> skimming bare trees
> above a snow glaze. (CWP1, 152)

Age's energy is thus eked out along the close-hugged flight path of "cheep*ing*-skimm*ing*"—the birds still holding off from descent to the "snow glaze" when,

> Gaining and failing
> they are buffeted
> by a dark wind—
> But what?

—a "wha*t*?" of "buff*eted*" hurt, perhaps; a deathly blow? But the poem keeps its syntactic suspense, and age's birds their live initiative. Brought closer to the earth, yet still not downfallen,

> On harsh weedstalks
> the flock has rested,
> the snow
> is covered with broken
> seedhusks

—the latter no Prufrockian waste of empty oyster shells, but more like the "White feathers in the snow" dashed down by the adventurous birds in the winds of "Gerontion." For after the "dark wind" threatening age in Williams's poem, the seedhusks signal replenishment, as the poem moves from "has rested" to "is covered" to

> the wind tempered
> by a shrill
> piping of plenty.

More than any "cheeping," the "piping" resounds with a last surprise: the "shrill" exulting of those who know what, in their time, they have joyously, abundantly eaten.

But as winter gradually yields to a new season in the first poem of *Spring and All*, Williams's control of pace, and his refusal to let remissions appear prematurely, have a greater strictness:

> By the road to the contagious hospital
> under the surge of the blue
> mottled clouds driven from the
> northeast—a cold wind. Beyond, the
> waste of broad, muddy fields
> brown with dried weeds, standing and fallen (CWP1, 177)

In its own visual unkemptness, the paragraph lets "the surge of the blue" spill over into "mottled," and broken-off definite articles raggedly connect with their nouns. But the arbitrary appearance is subject to the more severe command of the spoken poem—Williams only permitting the adverbial suggestion of a large, traveling onwardness ("By the road to . . . under the surge of . . . Beyond") while he actually keeps movement in a phrasal grip. Having brought back the clouds to a "driven" discipline (after "driving" forward too readily in the 1923 *Broom* version)[23] he ties the journeying suggestion to the bleak brevity of "a cold wind." Those "*blue / m*ottled clou*ds*" are equally held in an auditory kinship with "*broad, m*uddy fiel*ds*" as the "*broad . . . fields*" enclose "*brown . . . we*eds, standing and fallen"—the participles only a token reminder of what once moved (or might move again).

For with a verbless segment visually broken away from the mass of the first paragraph—

> patches of standing water
> the scatterings of tall trees

—there is hint of a less imprisoned energy. In this landscape of sparse, reused diction, the previous "standing" now belongs, as "standing water," with the small glints of acoustic vigor in "*p*at*c*hes" and "the s*catt*erings" of unfallen trees. More individualizings come, like spring's slow progress, in the next paragraph. There, still without a main verb, and again subject to no journeying but only an adverbial gesture ("All along the road . . .") the voice must press through dulling similarities ("*All al*ong . . . reddish / purplish") in order to pick out a "forked" distinctiveness:

> All along the road the reddish
> purplish, forked, upstanding, twiggy
> stuff of bushes and small trees
> with dead brown leaves under them
> leafless vines—

With "forked," one's pronunciation raises "*up*standing" out of previous "standings," just as it elicits by differentiation, after more layers of sameness ("dead brown *leaves* . . . *leaf*less vines"), what merely appears to be *"Lifeless"* in the two-line fragment following:

> Lifeless in appearance, sluggish
> dazed spring approaches—

Though it can be admitted, in "sluggish" hesitancy and with a finally permitted verb, that spring "approaches," verbs remain scarce, and must be carefully harbored in this bare word-terrain. Signs of spring's emergence are so gradual that the "dazed," semi-woken plants have no names at first. Only pronouns will suffice as

> They enter the new world naked
> cold, uncertain of all
> save that they enter.

—and *enter* more resolutely by the second use of that verb. Indeed, the force of their entering, rather than what occurs afterward, is Williams's focus. Two-line segments may look forward to "One by one" unfoldings:

> Now the grass, tomorrow
> the stiff curl of the wild carrot leaf

> One by one objects are defined—
> It quickens, clarity, outline of leaf

"But now," after the last line's hastening, Williams holds back in adherence to the unspeeded moment, as he sternly maintains the disciplined pace kept throughout:

> But now the stark dignity of
> entrance—Still, the profound change
> has come upon them; rooted, they
> grip down and begin to awaken

So, in "stark dignity," without the leafiness yet to come, "Still" exerts its power inside movement: the fixity that vouchsafes the awesome gradualness of "the profound change." In stately symmetry,

> Still . . .
> rooted . . .

and with toughness in that pinioning, the nameless plants may now, more resolutely, but no less unrushedly, "grip down and"—with growth's sure emphasis—"begin to *awaken*."

Again Williams's regulatory tact is supremely evident. With patience, and with Moore-like regard for Henry James's "differentiated . . . units of sound and sense,"[24] he can give voice to the muteness within unpromising ground. But Moore could never say with his kind of vehemence in the prose of *Spring and All* (written after the poems, in autumn 1922, and therefore contemporaneous with the publication of *The Waste Land*): "it is spring—both in Latin and Turkish, in English and Dutch, in Japanese and Italian; it is spring by Stinking River where a magnolia tree, without leaves, before . . . a ramshackle home for millworkers, raises its straggling branches of ivorywhite flowers."[25] For there Williams implicitly challenges Eliot's multilingual vistas and cruel April with a native season that can be translated into many tongues but remain itself: in his sense, the local universalized. At the same time, Williams's keen sympathy for all that grows defiantly in a hostile terrain or a culturally inhospitable America would seem to be expressed by the magnolia tree, akin to the "desert flower with roots under the sand of his day," as he describes Poe in *In the American Grain*:[26] a critical force bursting out from beneath his age's dead layers.

Eliot also observed the "starved environment" and "desert soil" in which Poe, Hawthorne, and Melville labored,[27] but as a poet whose own upward striving out of the seeming aridity of *The Waste Land* brings him especially close to Williams. The scene is not specifically American, and Eliot's resilience, unlike Williams's exuberance, must push its way out from under a greater weight of muteness, torpor, anguish, disgust, and dread. But it is a capacity for endurance, a shared compatriot stamina, which links the tree with "straggling branches" by Stinking River to the outreach of desire in "The Burial of the Dead": "What are the roots that clutch, what branches grow / Out of this stony rubbish?" (CPP, 61). Instead of deafly regarding these words as a cry of despair and scorn in a poetic *Decline of the West*, one can hear in the lift of the question a search for upspringing possibility—the voice and voices of the poem moving beyond personal misery and previous inhibition ("No, I am not Prince Hamlet") to the soundscapes and metamorphoses of a different Shakespearean prince.

These indeed are the rangings of the unfixed poetic self, the outsider in the European scene and America. Yet by going further from a homeland than Williams and Moore in their own necessary distancings, Eliot, for all the emotional cost, is then most intently native—not by harking back to American shores, as in the Boston "nighttown" sequence of the draft, "He Do the Police in Different Voices," but, as in the first lines of "The Burial of the Dead," by feeling his way into unspecified ground with the divining care shown by Williams. The latter's nameless plants "enter the new world naked" but Eliot can name his shoots when, by a participial probing of dormancies—

> breeding
> Lilacs out of the dead land, mixing

> Memory and desire, stirring
> Dull roots with spring rain (CPP, 61)

—he begets a shift of season and pace. Time is on the move, like the seaward river later in the poem. With the pulse of such currents, Eliot sounds out the rhythms and resources, the pluralities and singularities, that now, at risk of overflow—yet vitally so—enter the speech of *The Waste Land*.

Three

Sounding *The Waste Land*

The descent beckons
      as the ascent beckoned
WILLIAMS, "The Descent"

We should not be misled, especially by Eliot himself. Attempting to make the separate pieces of *The Waste Land* seem coherent at the simplest level, he told the reader in an endnote that Tiresias is "the most important personage in the poem, uniting all the rest." By also saying specifically that Mr. Eugenides "melts into the Phoenician sailor," and that the latter is "not wholly distinct from Ferdinand Prince of Naples," while "all women are one woman, and the two sexes meet in Tiresias"—a would-be conflation of distinctly separate speakers, moods, and energies into one world-weary and supposedly all-seeing "personage"—he opened the way, helped by his invocation of fertility myths, to the kind of critical commentary which pays no heed to the poem as a spoken revelation in moment-by-moment discovery. We are long used, after all, to depictions of *The Waste Land* as a structure of multifold allusiveness and cultural density reaching far beyond the local experience of the text. What words *are*, in auditory immediacy, matters distinctly less than what they stand for. So David Walker, for instance, in *The Transparent Lyric*, has a confident critical tradition behind him when he declares that the poem, with its "mythic scaffolding of Fisher King and the Grail Quest," is "governed by an essentially Symbolistic poetic,"[1] thus concurring with Marjorie Perloff in *The Poetics of Indeterminacy* who accepts Eliot's suggested merging of the figures and finds that "the symbolic threads are woven and designed so intricately that the whole becomes a reverberating echo chamber of meanings."[2]

Tracing these reverberations, however, is not the same as hearing the poem's actual acoustics—the voices of an unfolding psychic drama, defined through a sound-collage of historic memories and sequentially unfolded through line-by-line strivings. But then it is just as true to say that the later Eliot of *Four Quartets* eventually ceased to hear them himself. By 1946, when he came to record *The Waste Land*—a work that then probably seemed to him as emotionally remote as was "Black Earth" to the older Moore—he could even assume the vocal aloofness of a Tiresias and speak in the tones of monotonous fatalism as he moved through the poem at graveyard pace.[3] He had seemingly long forgotten what was once so immediate to him in the poem's original dar-

ing resonances when he first read the poem to friends in June 1922. Then "He
sang it & chanted it[,] rhythmed it," says Virginia Woolf,[4] intimating the vocal
variety and energy which characterize (without the singing) Eliot's virtually
unknown and only recently published recording of the poem at Columbia
University in 1933.[5]

It is the Columbia reading, so different from the 1946 version, which de-
serves particular attention because it directs us not only to Eliot's fresher,
vocalized investment in the poem but to the possibilities of *our* spoken reading. His speed of delivery at vital moments, as well as his passion and urgency, make audible what is there to be elicited and uttered from within the
verse-paragraphs, not imposed from the outside, by any speaker alert to the
rhythmic cues of anguish and recovery, or the vindictive and the tender. Eliot's extraordinary rendering acts especially as the pointer to the necessary
energy that a reader's voice must bring to capacious verse-sequences that have
to be ridden in dexterous continuity without letting them break apart: a persistence bringing us close to the way the poet himself assimilates the broken
and degraded into a height of style without being pulled down. It is the agility
by which the pronunciations of the speaker-reader follow the various routes
by which Eliot the outsider goes on to invigorate standard English via foreign languages and fragmentary music—whether German, French, American
English, Cockney English, Latin, Italian, Sanskrit, Wagnerian opera, Shakespearean lyric, Jacobean madrigal, ragtime tune, prophylactic jingle, nursery
rhyme, or the song of birds.

From the poem's beginning, however, the speaker is bound to the starts,
stops, and awakenings that the poem demands as a temporal succession.
"*Su*mmer *su*rprised us," say the anonymous sleepers of the earth, suddenly
made emergent, syllable jolting syllable, in a specific time and place. For
"Summer surprised us, coming over the Starnbergersee / With a shower of
rain," and though a more broad-spanning interpretation might connect such
water to a fertilizing of modernity's barren soil, it is the sounded-out name of
the German lake, "*Sh*tan-bearger-tsay," giving fresh distinctness to "*sh*ower"
and "*st*opped," which more immediately energizes the scene. But the acoustic
awakening must still resist lethargy's drone, because "stopped" also signals a
slowdown in pace by the dawdling "Ands" of a post-1918 leisured class:

> we stopped in the colonnade,
> And went on in sunlight, into the Hofgarten,
> And drank coffee, and talked for an hour.
> Bin gar keine Russin, stamm' aus Litauen, echt deutsch (CPP, 61)

Against the idle English tones, therefore (with their "in-on" halts: "*in* the col-
*onn*ade . . . *on* in . . . *in*to") come the German woman's staccato bursts, so assertive of her nationality amidst dislocation (with Eliotic sympathy here) that

the reader's voice is sped on again (with "stamm'" as agitative as "Starn-") to
the more urgent-sounding English of Marie and her Austrian memories. Ea-
gerly nonstop, the keen remembrance of "*ch*ildren" and an "ar*ch*-du*ke*" from a
prewar age ("e*ch*t deut*sch*" sharpening the tongue) sweeps aside the previous
"Ands" of the time-dulling talkers:

> And when we were children, staying at the arch-duke's,
> My cousin's, he took me out on a sled,
> And I was frightened. He said, Marie,
> Marie, hold on tight. And down we went.
> In the mountains, there you feel free.
> I read, much of the night, and go south in the winter.

Frightened adulthood applies the brake at the paragraph's end: "I read,"—with
comma's hesitancy—"much of the night,"—as speech briefly pauses on another comma—"and go south in the winter." But before all shuts down, Marie's
memory has excitedly moved "*out* on a sled" ("*aus* Lit*auen*" prompting the
way) as "*sled*" connects, without fear, to what "He *said*" and the heartening
words of close-huddled kinship: "Marie, / Marie, hold on tight. And *down* we
went." So, with fast, emphatic relish, they plunge to a descent and thereby rise
to the heights. "In the mountains"—the adverbial phrase coming first, to catch
the voice's exultant stress—"*there* you feel free."

But where exhilaration collapses into fear, or somnolence is startled into
life, Eliot's post-"Gerontion" paragraph demands of the speaker more than
modulating dexterity across three- to four-stress lines and abruptly shifting
contours. Equally crucial are the separate identities one's reading must give
to those voices of the poem who reach out to others in ambiguous or direct
human kinship—whether it is Marie's cousin ("hold on tight") or the desert
prophet, softening his grand, castigatory address to "Son of man" with a sinister whisper ("I will show you fear in a handful of dust") or, in the last section
of "The Burial of the Dead," the boisterous "I" of flesh-and-blood plausibility who interrupts the dream-march of the City of London clerks and cries
"Stetson!" Evolving as a single speaker from his spectral multiplication in the
Baudelaire poem "Les Sept Vieillards,"[6] and from acoustic submergence "*Un*-
der the brown fog" of the "*Un*real City" (or "Fourmillante cité"), he is moving
out of Dantescan grief ("so many, / I had not thought death had undone so
many") as the repetitive downbeat becomes the larger, *up*-down arc—"Flowed
up the hill and down King William Street"—by which he springs into prominence, "There," at the exact place and time where "Saint Mary Woolnoth kept
the hours / With a dead sound on the final stroke of nine." This is the "*I . . . I*"
at the clang of "n*i*ne," after "f*i*nal," who jauntily challenges death's burials:

> There I saw one I knew, and stopped him, crying, "Stetson!
> You who were with me in the ships at Mylae!

That corpse you planted last year in your garden,
Has it begun to sprout? Will it bloom this year?

Loud with the sharpness of "*St*arnbergersee," the noise of "*st*opped him, crying '*St*etson!'" has the credibility of one man hailing another across a London
street while at the same moment, with no overblown rhetoric, greeting a comrade across the centuries. Indeed, the more Eliot insists on the un-nonsensical
style of address, man to man, the more he can expand its outline with the
increasingly fantastic. So a big, flaunted casualness ("That corpse you planted . . .") maintains the shape of comradely speech while the upraised note
of questions ("sprout? . . . bloom?") tauntingly lifts into consideration a buried body—anthropologically a reminder of vegetation rites, but dramatical-
ly, face to face, the outrageously merry tormenting of the Crippen-like (but
fashionably-hatted) Stetson,[7] with his murderous secret. Animal mockery,
or the jeer of a deformed sexuality, strikes home with the insidious jollity of
a song from *The White Devil*, revised with an extra-"friendly" rhyme: "Oh
keep the Dog far h*e*nce, that's fri*e*nd to m*e*n, / Or with his nails he'll dig it
up ag*ai*n!"[8] But, as with the jibing subversion and sexual undermining of
Lil by another supposed friend in the pub scene of "A Game of Chess," the
pseudo-amicable framework can be stretched without over-warping. Thus the
paragraph sunk at the start in Baudelairean dream and dirty fog ends on a
higher Baudelairean note in the clear-cut syllables and dualistic feelings that
extend beyond the scene to "You," the page-reader, with a wilder fraternalism
and attack: "You! hypocrite lecteur!—mon semblable,—mon frère!"

Screeching the last word in his 1933 recording, Eliot goes on to read the first
paragraph of "A Game of Chess" at an amazingly fast pace. But for oneself, as a
speaking "lecteur" of the poem, the justification for such a reading already exists in the fraternal-scornful upsurge of Stetson's comrade. However twisted,
that partly articulates a desire to reach out of solitude toward another—a her-
alding of the inchoate force self-imprisoned by the *objets* of a luxurious room
("The Chair she sat in, like a burnished throne / Glowed on the marble"). For
there, however thwarted by a willfulness, amidst such pseudo-regal heights,
something genuine, in latter-day Prufrockism, is trying to speak and move.
So, even though the Shakespearean queen's river journey may be landlocked
in a stony pastiche which glows rather than burns, the energy is not static,
as the long, unbroken sentence strivingly makes clear. If the whole sequence
is not to collapse, like a psyche kept together by luxurious decor, one must
read it aloud with speed and carefully harbored breath. Strenuously upholding
such prolongation and the "Held-up" synthetic linkages of this claustrophobic
room, one must compulsively go on and on,

where the glass
Held up by standards wrought with fruited vines

> From which a golden Cupidon peeped out
> (Another hid his eyes behind his wing)[9]
> Doubled the flames of sevenbranched candelabra

where, in acoustic doubling and an extra burden for the voice, "seven*branched* candela*bra*" are

> Reflecting light upon the table as

—"*as*" rising on the upstress to make the next concocted link with "*rose*"—

> as
> The glitter of her jewels rose to meet it,
> From satin cases poured in rich profusion.

The reader, like Eliot in 1933, will have just enough breath left to pour out those jewels at the sentence's end, before imprisoned speech strives again for something humanly higher out of the room's erotic artifices. But what is so *under*neath ("*Un*stopped . . . perfumes, / *Un*guent, powdered, or liquid," like "*Un*real City, / *Un*der the brown fog") can only rise odorously to a closed-in "coffered ceiling." It is a further limiting height set on the upward urge by the picture from Ovid's *Metamorphoses*, "Above the antique mantel." But in the picture's "antique" version of the raped and humanly tongueless Philomela, the woman-turned-bird, an undefiled sound starts up from her silencing:

> there the nightingale
> Filled all the desert with inviolable voice
> And still she cried, and still the world
> Pursues, "Jug jug" to dirty ears

Despite the vulgar rapacity which turns an innocent madrigal's words ("Pretty wantons, sweetly sing . . . Jug, jug, tereu tereu")[10] into the mechanistic "Jug jug" of lustful demand, the metamorphosed Philomela will not be silenced by a muffling sexuality. Opening out from "nightingale" to "*all*" to "inviolable" in the poetic exile's desert, the "inviolable voice" of a potentially *echt* human speech, becoming naturalized in Eliot's place of dispossession, shakes the boundary of the expensive room and its fakeries. The "still . . . still" of Philomela's pain demands motion not stasis, as the woman's brushed hair "Glowed into words, then would be savagely still": the savagery just held back at the paragraph's end so that her actual words erupt with extra frenzy in the next paragraph: "My nerves are bad to-night. Yes, bad. Stay with me. / Speak to me." As with Stetson's comrade, plain-speaking plausibility coexists with the fantastic: her wilder staccato jabs ("Speak . . . What thinking? What? . . . Think") matching in bizarre bits the smooth, strange raptness of her companion/husband's answer: "I think we are in rat's alley / Where the dead men lost their bones." But while that entranced tone drifts off to desolation's phantasmagoria, the woman's un-mystical demand, "What is that noise?," instantly pulls the situation back to a here-and-now urgency—aggravated by his leisurely dream-answers ("Those are pearls that were his eyes . . .") to demand in final rapidity: "Are you alive, or not? Is there nothing in your head?" Her voice drives their separate fates, and lines, toward a joint, manic imprisonment or verse-block. But, or

But

—as his word hangs portentously alone in the text, with a grand, lingering upstress—the brake on her speed is only the prelude to the extra, astonishing frivolity of his:

> O O O O that Shakespeherian Rag—
> It's so elegant
> So intelligent
> "What shall I do now? What shall I do?
> I shall rush out as I am, and walk the street
> With my hair down, so. What shall we do tomorrow?
> What shall we ever do?"

There is no release, even though the "O's" welling up from underground would seem to betoken something spontaneously uncalculated. They have the breath, instead, of a mock-exaltation which turns the title of the 1912 lyric "That Shakespearean Rag"—syllabically well-rounded and carefree on "Shakespearean"—into the jerkily aspirate.[11] A clipped caricature of syncopation supplants the Rag's wording ("Most intelligent, very elegant") with "so ele-gant / So in-telli-gent": a stiffening just-so-ness of decorum (after So-so-stris's being "so careful these days," Philomela's being "So rudely forced," and the London crowd's "so many") which thwarts the neurotic woman's desire to rush out "With my hair down, so." Letting go—*so* deliberately—is thus frantic illusion: a downfall, after so much reaching for the heights, and an imprisonment in despair of time: "What shall we *ever* do?"

Yet descent can also be a means to rhythmic ascent and recovery. Where the poet's own Swiss convalescence has a part in the poem ("By the waters of Leman I sat down and wept")[12] recuperation is an upward striving: the movement that eventually leads the speaking voice out of anguish, scorn, and fear to the great tidal swell of "The Fire Sermon." But these cleansing currents owe nothing to Tiresias in that part, the observer of the typist-clerk episode, and installed, like Sosostris's tarot cards, as a unifying device. Disparager of the "low," whether it is the clerk ("One of the low on whom assurance sits / As a silk hat on a Bradford millionaire") or "the lowest of the dead," walked among in past ages, the supposed all-surveying Tiresias is left behind in his static loftiness by the humbler, evolving voice of *The Tempest*'s Ferdinand: the figure who begins his rise from desolation in "The Fire Sermon" as the anonymous "I" who asks "Sweet Thames" to "run softly." Quieting the bones' sinister "*rattle*" in his mind, as "A *rat* crept softly through the vegetation," he becomes more identifiably a princely fisher "in the dull canal" and the voice of patient forbearance. Just as Shakespeare's character piles up his logs without complaint and rises above the mean task to which Prospero has subjected him, Eliot's Ferdinand ascends from baseness—slightly higher than the belly-dragging rat and just above a now-allayed disgust at sexual animality (or "rat's alley / Where the dead men lost their bones")—by modestly placing, line by line, as the speaking voice discovers, one piece of ruin "upon" another: "Musing upon the king my brother's wreck / And on the king my father's death before him." Meditatively, rhythmically, and gradually he is establishing without Tiresian superiority a small lineage of height above a lowness ("White bodies naked on a low damp ground") which, reiterated ("And bones cast in a little low dry garret") is letting him cast away, unextravagantly, any lingering sense of horror about the bone beneath the flesh. The "ga*rret*" clinks out the bones' fright merely, "*Rattl*ed by the *rat*'s foot only, year by year": a line of such resurgent confidence, as one reads it aloud, that this "I" can truly be said, with the poem's time sense rhymingly redeemed from emptiness, to have outlasted "year to year" what once spread "from ear to ear" as a wintry chuckle. What was the sound of backbiting betrayal ("But at my back in a cold blast . . .") has been surpassed by the chime of a different season:

> But at my back from time to time I hear
> The sound of horns and motors, which shall bring
> Sweeney to Mrs. Porter in the spring.
> O the moon shone bright on Mrs. Porter
> And on her daughter
> They wash their feet in soda water
> *Et O ces voix d'enfants, chantant dans la coupole!*

Ascent, not fall, is the exuberant effect. Indeed, more gusto rather than a sardonic note of bathos and banality is demanded of the speaking voice, as the iambics of Ferdinand's Marvellian modesty ("from time to time I hear") launch a four-beat surprise in the outspread "sound of horns and motors, which shall bring" (with uplifted expectancy at the line-break) an apeneck Actaeon to a brothel Diana: all without a collapse into deflating irony. For in this modern rite of spring, the spoken zest of Ferdinand-Eliot (forbidding any Tiresias-Eliot scorn for the "low") takes such impulse in its undisgusted stride. From horns and motors to the moon-high merriment of the foot-washing song, delight is impelled higher by mechanical instigations, as the abrupt rhymes of "Mrs. Por-*ter*" and "her daugh-*ter*," doubled by "so-*da* wa-*ter*," together with insistently hard, iambic segments ("Thĕy wásh—thĕir féet—ǐn sód—ǎ wát—ěr") provide the push that lifts the princely voice to the new fluency of the line from Verlaine's "Parsifal." As Charles Tomlinson observes, this recalls the purity of the boys' voices singing high up in the dome of the Holy Grail in Wagner's opera.[13] Thus, higher than the failed exultance of the Shakespearean Rag's "O's," and gaining an upsurge from the full-breathed roundness of "O the moon shone bright," Ferdinand's "O ces voix" marks the summit of his step-by-step rise to the unaborted melody of those "enfants, chantant dans la coupole."

It is also the music of a resilience in the poem. Eliot has created through Ferdinand the stretchable vocal outline that has more princely Shakespearean definition than the expandable confines of "Gerontion," and more importance as an assimilating voice than his mythic role as the Fisher King in waiting. "[N]ot indeed a 'character,'" as an endnote says of Tiresias, yet reaching out to others without Tiresian disdain, this "I" who began without exaltation just above the creeping rat, and climbed to *"ces voix"* by means of Mrs. Porter's mechanistic song, can absorb the automatic sameness of the typist putting a record "on" the gramophone and build "upon" it. Death is not the memory ("Those are pearls that were his eyes") but the incremental sound of a different Shakespearean song:

"This music crept by me upon the waters"
And along the Strand, up Queen Victoria Street.
O City city, I can sometimes hear

It is only "sometimes" (like the modesty of "from time to time") but that is the ungrandiose persistence which can track a way eastward through the dull, metrical thoroughfare of "Queen Victoria Street" to a City (humbly scaled back to a lowercase "city") where the voice's down-thudding tread to "a public bar in Lower Thames Street" is no obstacle to an ear which enjoys there "The pleasant whining of a mandoline." If "whin*ing*" is aurally made pleasant for Eliot in both recordings by his Italian-style pronunciation of "mandol*een*" (after "mandolino") so also cacophonous "clatter" is rhymingly eased with "chatter" in the pub "Where fishmen lounge at noon" and where, as the lines build toward—aurally *build* the columns of—the riverside church in Lower Thames Street,

                                        the walls
Of Magnus Martyr hold
Inexplicable splendour of Ionian white and gold.

By that last extended line—balancing the heave of "Inexplicable splendour" by "Ionian" resonance—Wren's spaced-out architecture finds its vocal equivalence. So, with "*spl*endour" disentangled from "Ine*x*plicable," and "*I-o*-nian" opening up the luminous vowels of "wh*i*te and g*o*ld," a vigorous continuity carries over in the change from a lengthy verse-line to small, terse segments, as if the princely voice were still there, but transformed. For what is *"white"* so positively, in Ferdinand's purifying exultance, ensures that "The river *sweats* / Oil and tar," not as the lax verb of pollution's drift but of decisive, cleansing exertion:

> The river sweats
> Oil and tar
> The barges drift
> With the turning tide
> Red sails
> Wide
> To leeward, swing on the heavy spar.

By taut, out-pushing tenacity, rather than languor, the lines require, whether in Eliot's rapid 1933 reading or ours, that "*ba*rges" should not let "*tar*" lie, but be freshly re-echoed in "the *tur*ning tide." With that turn, "Red sails" do not hang lifelessly but, in a curt thrust against the rhyme with "tide," swivel harder, "*Wi*de / To lee*ward*." The Ferdinand "I" may not be explicitly here, but the "*whi*te and gold" of his voice persists in "*wi*de" and "s*wi*ng," with the accompanying chorus of "*Wei*lalala leia" (a German *v* for *w*) from Wagner's Rhine-maidens, naturalized on the Thames. However, they are not singing tragically from *Götterdämmerung*, as Eliot's endnote would suggest, but, as Tomlinson observes, from *Das Rheingold* before their gold is stolen.[14] Without lament, therefore, a music of possibility (the later "awful daring of a moment's surrender") beats with the maidens' "*leia . . . leialala*" underneath the river memory of "Elizabeth and *Lei*cester / Beating oars"—not a futile historical deadlock but, in the spirit of Spenser's *Epithalamion*, the rhythm of potential wedded intimacy, "on the spot," as Eliot's note makes clear. Whatever the encrusting of lost opportunity in the royal barge's "gilded shell," a princely momentum carries the "shell" forward on the "swell":

> The brisk swell
> Rippled both shores
> Southwest wind
> Carried down stream
> The peal of bells
> White towers

Even as the speaking reader moves from the Ferdinand vocal outline to the individual, non-chorus voices of the Thames-daughters, the sense of the prince's underlying resilience is not lost. What "*Ri*ppled both shores" with such "*bri*sk" provocation, and lets the "*wi*nd" resound in "*Whi*te towers" before the fade-away on "*Wei*alala leia," continues in the temporary shift back from seagoing freshness. The tune of the river swell is still here—"Wallala" on the upsurge, and "leialala" in descent—when, within its wide arc, the next line, "Trams and dusty trees"—the first daughter's re-siting of the scene—also rises and falls in miniature. It is the uncomplaining rhythm inside the larger, non-elegiac movement whereby the small ascent to degradation ("By Richmond I raised my knees") flattens in neutral acceptance, "Supine on the floor of a narrow canoe." With the second daughter's implied emphasis, it is "My *feet*," rather than a regretful self, which "are at Moorgate, and my heart" (rising at the line-end in possible grief) "Under my feet" (in firm downgrading of such a possibility). "What should *I* resent?" she asks, again with implicit stress, as the seaward movement, halted "On Margate Sands" brings us to a final daughter, bereft of a personal "I." In her disconnection from "The broken fingernails of dirty hands," it is the rising expectancy of others, not herself, which builds in the verse-line ("My people humble people who expect . . .") and falls to the calm of "Nothing": a small, emotional bareness, rather than bitter nullity, sung to by the now hardly audible "la la" of the river chorus.

Against that, in the sudden voice change demanded by a single, assertive line—

To Carthage then I came

—the individualized "I" returns with the force of Augustine. But as the Christian clamorously intrudes into the unresentful mood—damning City lust with his "Burning burning burning burning," and grandly insistent on his personal salvation ("O Lord Thou pluckest me out") yet left clutching at the air ("O Lord Thou pluckest")—a more softly spoken energy is reinvigorated. What began neither "loud or long" in Ferdinand's climb to recovery, and which can still be just heard in the reticence of "Nothing," is the core of precise, undeceived feeling that, after the pause on the page after Augustine, is to be spoken as a quiet yet differently fired "burning." Neither the sensuality condemned by the saint, nor the flames of the transitory invoked by the Buddha's Fire Sermon, this, with Ferdinand-like modesty, is the small, unclamorous yearning to go up again, whether through phantasmagoria or the concrete, physical world.

It is the mood continued by the Phoenician sailor in "Death by Water": not a figure who "melts" into Mr. Eugenides and others but who, in his distinct way, partakes of the Thames daughters' rise-and-fall rhythm and the vital quieting where his bones are "Picked in whispers." Unexorbitant sound goes on, moreover, to acquire a special authority in the first paragraph of "What the Thunder Said" after the big, historical noise, "The shouting and the crying / Prison and palace and reverberation," which marks the death of pagan and Christian gods. With everything quieted down to those "now dying / With a little patience," the plain, humble note is the foundation for further upward striving:

> Here is no water but only rock
>
> Rock and no water and the sandy road
> The road . . .

Eliot in 1933 reads fast, as if relentlessly driven, and one is reminded of the rapidity needed for the earlier paragraph, "The Chair she sat in," so that the on-and-on connectiveness does not flag. The same holds true here where the text encourages one's own speedy delivery, as the nonstop anadiplosis demand (the last noun of one line repeated in the next) chains "rock" to "Rock" and makes "the sandy road" inescapably

> The road winding above among the mountains
> Which are mountains of rock without water

—a binding together of the acoustic linkages "*above among*," with no relief from sameness, "*among* . . . the *mou*ntains of rock with*out* water." This is to be thirst-maddened in the flesh as much as the spirit, with the solidity that derives from Vachel Lindsay's poem, "What the Miner in the Desert Said": "If I could climb the ridge and drink . . . If I could drain that keg":[15]

> If there were water we should stop and drink
> Amongst the rock one cannot stop or think

—a crazed onwardness as speech is deliriously choked with stone ("Dead *mou*ntain *mou*th of carious teeth that cannot spit") where the "*carious*," exasperatingly, "*cannot*."

Yet in this hell a new, short-line paragraph lets sanity breathe again. At each line-end, the mind's voice *can* stop and think:

> If there were water
>
> And no rock
>
> Adjusting the wish—
>
> If there were rock
> And also water

— desire finds the key to the next line—

> And water

—where the reality of water seems to be urging its way up from deep springs within the self. In the short, eager bursts that the lines demand ("And water—A spring—A pool among the rock") the "sound of water" actually seems to lead (if only the impulse can be sustained with the right integrity, and one's voice can uphold a mounting delight) past thought of "the cicada / And dry grass singing" to "sound of water over a rock," where "over" ascends to "Where the hermit-thrush sings in the pine trees." As with the Philomela nightingale—the animal sense raised to its keenest, untainted level—it is the clean, inviolable song to which human words aspire in attunement, as the speaker moves, "Drip drop drip drop," in concordant rise and fall, with the bird's waterlike chords and tremolo. Then, in separate pieces, "drop drop drop," the fluid imagining falls away, unable to sustain the upwardness any further. "But there *is* no water," as the plain fact must be stressed at the paragraph's end.

That, however, is the sound of a clarity which is scouring the mind of its terrors. The "hooded" phantom on another mountain road; the "hooded hordes swarming / Over endless plains," together with the "Who's" and "What's" of unanswered questions flailing in the void: all are left behind, together with "Falling towers" and "Unreal" cities, by the poem's movement through the "*whisp*er music" (bizarrely fiddled on a woman's drawn-out hair) to the "bats with baby faces" who more more loudly "*Whist*led, and beat their wings." Crawling "head *down*ward *down* a blackened wall," the childlike creatures of imagination's plunge ("And down we went . . .") lift the plagued mind on the iambics' upstress ("Ånd úp—sĭde dówn—iň áir—wĕre tów–ĕrs")—those "*towers*" not collapsing but re-steadied against discord as the bells chimingly keep "the h*ours*," while voices, with the same wide-vowelled openness, are "singing *out* of" (not trapped inside) "empty cisterns and exhausted wells."

It is an upsoaring that brings the speaking voice to another bird on high— the French cock "on the roof tree" of the empty Christian chapel whose rat-a-tat speed ("Co co rico co co rico") immediately vivifies the English that follows, "In a flash of lightning."[16] Forecasting rain, the sound also looks forward (now that Christianity, the Buddha, and the pagan gods have been left behind) to the "DA" of Hindu scripture in the poem's final paragraph and the last mountain of "What the Thunder Said." But as one vocally climbs from "Ganga was s*un*ken" to the "h*um*ped," silent jungle to "Then spoke the thunder," no vast resonance follows. For despite its capital-letter prominence on the page, "DA" (as is clear from the moral logic of the passage, and as Eliot suggests by the softly breathed vowel of his 1933 recording) needs no superhuman crash. In earthly wisdom rather than transcendent might, the Hindu Lord of Creation is addressing his students on the principles of human conduct with the open-ended sound of "DA" which must be made terrestrially specific by the closed consonants of "*Datta*" ("Give")—the instantly rapped Sanskrit which sharpens with urgency the English question demanding an answer: "what have we given? / My friend, blood shaking my heart / The awful daring of a moment's surrender . . ." And memory of that keen moment, defying prudence's retractions, must be kept by the fast-paced pressure of the voice ("*this, and*"—with stressed repetition—"this *only*") that allows no deathly faltering:

> By this, and this only, we have existed
> Which is not to be found in our obituaries
> Or in memories draped by the beneficent spider
> Or under seals broken by the lean solicitor
> In our empty rooms

Breath, pushing its way through cobwebbed endings and imprisoning "in's" ("in our obituaries . . . in memories . . . In our empty rooms") only just expires at the sentence's end before it is revived by another "DA" and the immediately following *Dayadhvam* ("Sympathize"). Like "*Himavant*" earlier, with its rumbling suggestion of "imminent," "-*ayadhv*am" provokes without halt its unscrambled English implication: "*I have* heard the key / Turn in the door once and turn once only." That would be the auditory chance to act right away on a lock-opening impulse ("once only") in the exit from the self's prison toward sympathetic relation, rather than letting the mind—as the verse ponderingly slows down—turn the lock upon us: "each in his prison / Thinking of the key." Such thinking lets the sound of singleness's "only" trail away to a darkening mereness in "Only at nightfall" as archaic noise ("rumours") is heard from a historical distance, and "aethereal rumours / Revive for a moment a broken Coriolanus" (the child-hero who boasted in his ruin, "Alone I did it").[17] Yet it is the heart's larger daring beyond the uniquely alone, in an outreach to others, which the final "DA" revives:

> DA
> *Damyata*: The boat responded
> Gaily, to the hand expert with sail and oar

Damyata ("Control") ensures immediately that "The *boat* responded," not a solitary self; and "responded / Gaily," (with a comma's pause on that exact joyousness) to the "hand" of command rather than loose and wandering emotion. Guided here by accurate zest, not turbulence, one belongs to a momentum greater than the self, or could so nearly have belonged to it, in the seized instant. There, where "The sea was calm," (with another comma's halting of excess onrush) "your heart would have responded / Gaily, when invited": such warmth of invitation that the "heart," rather than "you," in this intimate-impersonal directness, seems already, with pleasurable order, to be "*beating* obedient / To controlling hands."

All the more surprising, then, after the verse seems to sail forward, are the brakes on advance set by the voice of the returned, landbound Ferdinand in the final paragraph. But Eliot's characteristic pull-back ("I sat upon the shore"—in enjambed deliberation—"Fishing,"—a comma's slight hesitation— "the arid plain behind me") is the desultory cover by which he launches the most startling forward thrust of the entire poem. The auditory Fisher King suddenly plunges from adult diffidence and unambitious musing ("Shall I at least set my lands in order?") to nursery rhyme glee—"London Bridge is falling down falling down falling down"—in another childlike descent ("And down we went") but also with the fast patter of a different rule as the voice of English (and the potentially inhibited mind) finds freedom, pronunciation's metamorphoses, and a new sequential meaning in the acoustic linkages of non-English fragments.

Entering the Italian of *Purgatorio* ("*Poi s'ascose nel foco che gli affina*": translatable as "Then he dived into the fire which refines him"), Ferdinand and vocal reader are also translated, not with over-fast pace but with the upward leap of intonation on the verb "*s'ascose*," the noun "*foco*" and the verb "*affina*," so as to connect with a longed-for transformation in the Latin of *Pervigilium Veneris* that follows: "*Quando fiam uti chelidon*." For if one's tongue picks up "*affina*" and transports it into "*fiam*," that is the same as winging the desire of the translated words ("When I shall be as the swallow") across from "chelidon" (the *o* as in "dome") to the cry of the lover in Tennyson's *The Princess* who yearns to be the bird on his mistress's lattice: "*O swallow swallow*." Ferdinand's princely fantasia rises on the open vowels, just as it descends from *The Princess* to the shut-in, nasalized despondency of de Nerval's inconsolable lover ("*Le Prince d'Aquitaine à la tour abolie*") and to an apparently hopeless shoring—imagination's boat equally beached in that sense—"ag*ai*nst" the gloom of "Aquit*ai*ne."

But in following out setback's acoustic insistences, one equally partakes of the Eliot-Ferdinand versatility that now hits back at despair by crazily erupting out of restraint: "Why then Ile fit you. Hieronymo's mad againe." The cry of Thomas Kyd's revenger (firstly abiding by the royal decorum of a "stately-written tragedy . . . fitting kings,"[18] then striking out with the implicit voice of *The Spanish Tragedy*'s "mad" yet silent subtitle)[19] has the mouth-widening challenge ("*Why . . . Ile*") and the Elizabethan lengthening "ag*ai*ne" (different from the /e/ of "dig it up ag*ai*n") which not only overrides "Aquitaine" but threatens to burst open the frame of linguistic multiplicity and its freeing sanity, which Ferdinand has held together, in exhilaration *and* command. However, at the point of greatest containment-breaking risk in all of Eliot's poetry, the sound of "m*a*d" is suddenly absorbed and arrested by the re-entering Sanskrit of "D*a*tta." The firmly reiterated principles, each halted for separate consideration—

Datta. Dayadhvam. Damyata.

—shape the repetition of a single word's calm in the even uniformity by which the poem's end has to be spoken:

Shantih shantih shantih

Glossed by Eliot's notes as "The Peace which passeth understanding," "Shantih" has several ways of being pronounced. When the three words are said together at the end of a Vedic hymn, the last is lengthened as "Shan-ti-hih."[20] When Eliot reads it in his 1946 recording, each trochaic "Shan tih" fades away into tranquility. But when he reads it in 1933 as an iambic, so that "Shăn tíh" has a "-tih" like "tick," as sharp-edged as the French bird's "Co co rico co co rico," he makes it the sound of waking up, not sleep: thus truest to the verse which, from "stamm' aus Litauen" to "Damyata," has startled the seeming dead into life, and nurtured the un-grandiose acoustic into resonant strength. Such is the water-speech which patience has struggled toward in desert and deadlock, in retreat and advance, as a river leads from city to sea, Europe to Asia, past to present. Such also is the way that Eliot, far from his native land but winning back lineages with a foreign, eclectic boldness, has become, in the end, a distinctly American voyager.

To Williams, however, he is an American renegade—at least in the public version of his complaint against The Waste Land. Decrying it as the abandonment of a project based on "local conditions" (where Moore is retrospectively recruited, against her wishes, as "a rafter holding up the superstructure of our uncompleted building"),[21] Williams, admittedly jealous,[22] almost certainly felt outshone as the poet of Spring and All by "the blast of Eliot's genius."[23] But where "blast" also has its acoustically bracing significance, in the disparate cries, songs, dissonances, and attunements of a regained solid world, cohering out of sickness and phantasmagoria by means of a princely speaker, it is not vexation that Eliot brings into relief but Williams's parallel resilience as the creator of extraordinary new wholes from fortuitously gathered pieces.

Out of a more easily loved—at times, too easily loved—multifoliate world Williams wrests his compositional designs. But in this effort, where Williams's onward dancing poise could be emotionally pulled down, Eliot's greater intensity, in seeking to win sane balance out of torments and repulsions, again provides a perspective. Behind the unsentimental impetus, the deft buoyancies, or the keen sympathies of the best verse in Spring and All lies the sense of all that might plunge accurate feeling into the mire of amorous allure, unarticulated desires, and furies. Williams's clear structures have to be won out of potential enthrallments, but his disengagings are thereby vitalized, as is suggested when he reviews Robert McAlmon's 1922 book of short stories A Hasty Bunch. There he observes how a student on a vacation job in one story is forced to row, after a Californian dam-burst, under brushwood's "smothering" and "swampy, sweating foliage" before he rejoins his nonchalant fellow-workers on dry land:[24] a clear example to Williams of an eventual winning-out, however dense the immersion. "It doesn't matter about being lost in a rowboat in a cotttonwood swamp" because "a free life of the intelligence" is "riding the flood."[25] One sees the peril of the openness, but also the possible prize, if, with sympathy's detachment rather than aloofness, mind and voice can be energized by inveiglements and profusions. Then Williams is no longer Eliot's resentful competitor but the poet who now embarks on his most audacious spoken adventure so far, as he rides the flood with his own sovereign sureness.

Four

Riding the Flood

"Here is a cold, modern style, bred of an attack capable of absorbing, not from a window but from the round of a circle in the open, anything in modern life pressing upon it."

WILLIAMS on McAlmon's prose[1]

Here, though, in *Spring and All*'s twenty-fourth poem, "The Avenue of Poplars," is a cool yet unfrigid bravura:

> I ascend
>
> through
> a canopy of leaves
>
> and at the same time
> I descend (CWP1, 228)

Up, down, in firmly declared poise, Williams is seemingly closer to Moore's "Black Earth" ("Now I breathe . . . now I am sub- / merged") than to Eliot's hard-earned climbs and descents. For, with the light matching of phrase to phrase, and a tone of teasing insouciance,

> I do nothing
> unusual—
>
> I ride in my car
> I think about
>
> prehistoric caves
> in the Pyrenees—
>
> the cave of
> *Les Trois Frères*

Yet "*Frères*" rasps with a fraternal welcome from the artist of modernity to the makers of the neolithic cave paintings, and Williams ("mon semblable,—mon frère!") cannot but suggest an equally contemporary kinship as he touches without acknowledgment the "mind of Europe," which in Eliot's 1919 essay "abandons nothing *en route*" and "does not superannuate either Shakespeare, or Homer, or the rock drawing of the Magdalenian draughtsmen."[2] Eliot can indeed be taken at his word as Williams brings the age-old paintings (discovered in 1914) into his artistic ancestry, while Moore brings into hers, through a 1921 poem, an ancient fish image which originates from the archaeological discovery of an Egyptian pulled bottle the year before.[3] But unlike her, Williams is keeping at bay a predilection for amorous fantasy. Even if the poem shows that "leaves embrace / in the trees" and that "Gypsy lips" seem "pressed" to his own, this car-rider is not to be swerved off course by allurements—at least for now.

However, for a man so concerned with "those things which lie under the direct scrutiny of the senses," there is difficulty in remaining detached from sensuous submergence while not insisting on an exaggerated distance from the world of physical desire. By an uneasy stridency, he asserts his disentanglement in "Young Love" (Poem IX)—"I: clean / clean / clean"—as if to exonerate himself from the clingings and immersions of a past affair ("Your sobs soaked through the walls / breaking the hospital to pieces": an image notably shared with Toomer's *Cane*).[4] But in "To Elsie" (XVIII) Williams stands apart from sexual enmeshings with the voice of ironic gusto that only reveals the greater emotional confusion overwhelming him: the un-transcendable sense of being sunk inside an alien land that has no genuine speech or focus. Lusts and inarticulate scatterings belong together when—satiric fanfare!—"The pure products of America / go crazy" in the placeless place where "young slatterns" are "bathed / in filth" and flaunt

> sheer rags—succumbing without
> emotion
> save numbed terror
>
> under some hedge of choke-cherry
> or viburnum
> which they cannot express— (CWP1, 217)

The only expressibility that can break into the repetitive, inarticulate hum of "suc*cum*bing," "*numb*ed," "*some*," and the acoustically *numb*ed "vibur*num*," occurs—but with more generalized "*some*s"—when there arrives at "some hard-pressed house . . . some doctor's family, some Elsie." Even so, Williams's housemaid, with her gangling body "addressed to cheap / jewelry," and taking the shoddy for the genuine, is merely "voluptuous water / expressing" with ironic muteness and "with broken // brain the truth about us"—the giddiness of dislocation in America that makes "the earth / under our feet" seem "an excrement of some" (only *some*) "sky." Williams's scornful throwaway is also part of the blurred language he cannot sharpen; for "*Some*how / it seems to destroy us" and though (with a gesture beyond the muting noise of the poem's "somes") "*some*thing is given off"; it is only in the last stanza that the language resounds with a clear-cut dignity:

> No one
> to witness
> and adjust, no one to drive the car.

The car of cultural blankness may be sent on a runaway ride, but with that second, vehemently repeated "*no* one," Williams begins to win back belated command of the verse-vehicle driven so confidently in "The Avenue of Poplars." This is not to be achieved, however, with the kind of open-ended freedom which impressed Marsden Hartley so much in the performances of the vaudeville equestrienne May Wirth that he imagined himself "your own perfect dada-ist . . . riding your own hobby-horse into infinity of sensation" and "into the wide expanse of magnanimous diversion."[5] For despite Williams seeing in Poem V "why / Hartley praises Miss Wirt" (*sic*), and despite having his own temporary sense of affinity with the Dadaism of Picabia and Duchamp,[6] he, like Eliot, in his necessary divergence from the Dadaist sound poets' abandonment of syntactic continuity, needs tight-channeled curbs to keep his freewheeling independence on track. This is particularly evident when he rides out again in "The Right of Way" (XI). Having recovered the balance so absent in "To Elsie," he is now moving through a land made utterable by a defter detachment which only retains its acuity through potential engrossment:

> In passing with my mind
> on nothing in the world
>
> but the right of way
> I enjoy on the road by
>
> virtue of the law—
> I saw (CWP1, 205)

Where "nothing in the world" has its carefree abandon lifted on the open vowels of "way," "enjoy," "by," and "virtue," the forward bounce of rhyme from "law" to "saw" would seem to maintain the frictionless push of stanza on stanza. But just as Moore's example shows Williams the importance of passing through "definite objects which give a clear contour to her force,"[7] so the birds' wings, as he notes in the *Spring and All* prose, "beat the solid air without which none could fly."[8] Thus the voice's right of way, kept un-garrulously on course by stanza trimness, is defined by the solid sight of

> an elderly man who

smiled and looked away

to the north past a house—
a woman in blue

who was laughing . . .

Impulsion after impulsion: one must catch a further breath at "house," before
the "woman in blue" (bringing the vowels of "who" and "looked" into overt
insistence) sends the voice, with another "who," into a network of further
looking. But just at the point where distraction beckons in so much joyous
intimacy—the woman's "laughing and / leaning forward to look up" into the
"half / averted face" of the man who has already looked away (and who, like
the poet, is half-turned aside from a potentially amorous closeness)—"a boy of
eight" (so emphatically) is also "looking" and pushing the voice on again, with
a further breath taken, to something more impersonal. For he is

looking at the middle of

the man's belly
at a watchchain—

and at the center of a composition that connects all the parts of this unex-
plained, personal scene. What had been the "vast import" claimed in "Pastoral" for the poor's creating a sense of locality out of haphazard pieces, has become for Williams, in such chanced-upon linkage, "The supreme importance
/ of this nameless spectacle." But the "*spec*tacle," undetainingly, is what also
"*sped*" him onwards, as the sentence and car

sped me by them
without a word—

Why bother where I went?
for I went spinning on the

four wheels of my car
along the wet road until

I saw a girl with one leg
over the rail of a balcony

Lifted past the group of man, woman, and boy, he is not going to be halted by
a more seductive pose. For having sped on "without a word" (or "with-o-u-t
a w-o-rd" in the mouth-stretched, unworried gusto that asks "*Why* bother
where I went?") he "*went* spinning" (in "*spinning*'s" imparted emphasis) "on
the four *wheels* . . . along the *wet* road": a ground-skimming momentum cut
into by the split pieces of textual beguilement ("a girl with one leg—over the

rail—of a balcony") but spurred on its way past angular geometry rather than allurement, as Williams's verve continues "over the rail of a balcony" and implicitly beyond it.

So he rides on through his land, neither floundering in submergence nor vaunting a clean detachment. Where Eliot's Ferdinand is not stuck in desolation or Tiresian aloofness, as he moves by leaps from the English City's "horns and motors" to *"ces voix"* of a higher song, Williams, with a style that equally seems "capable of absorbing anything in modern life pressing upon it," keeps his kind of nimble balance in the New York City journeyings of "Rapid Transit" (XXV). Here, however, he is not staving off a weight of fear and disgust like Eliot, but escaping over-fast aggression as he cries, "What the hell do you know about it?" in reply to the anti-poetry voice that barks: "To hell with you and your poetry— / You will rot and be blown / through the next solar system." The best answer to such contempt (and the mechanistic voice of deadly statistics: "Somebody dies every four minutes / in New York State—") is the healthier, slowed-down language of safety posters:

> Don't get killed
>
> Careful Crossings Campaign
> Cross Crossings Cautiously (CWP1, 231)

Rushing is prohibited by the extra-careful enunciations which separate word from word, but which then make possible a less hindered pace. For at a city advertisement's larger crossing-point

THE HORSES	black
	&
PRANCED	white

Just as Moore once demanded her own literary "space" as "a fit gymnasium for action," Williams's typography here asserts a monochrome right to *his* space in the city, while the voice, holding back for an instant on the animal subject, then jumping to the verb, strikes a way to the horse-pranced freedom of the open country. Poster cries ("Outings in New York City"; "Acres and acres of green grass / wonderful shade trees, rippling brooks") are reset within Williams's spacious layout on the page; but in the end it is more important that he should tell the passenger, without rippling cliché or "Acres" of superfluous words, concisely how to get there:

> Take the Pelham Bay Park Branch
> of the Lexington Ave. (East Side)
> Line and you are there in a few
> minutes

Interborough Rapid Transit Co.

Having shaped official directions into a visually trim verse-block, Williams can make them undertake a controlled vocal journey—not with a speediness mimicking the train itself (we remember the regulatory effect of "Overture to a Dance of Locomotives") but with the word-by-word steadiness that must cope with the plosive thud of the "Pelham Bay Park Branch" and the fully pronounced detail of the "Lexington Avenue (East Side) Line." Going not too rapidly by that route, the speaking voice has earned the comparative ease of the traveler's arrival, when "you are there in a few" (unimportantly added) "minutes." With rapidity braked in small pauses, but not halted, it is the verbal conveyance of passenger and reader by the "Interborough—Rapid Transit—Company."

Yet speedy ferocity was there at the start, and it is a measure of the force which Williams has to control that one hears a fast-moving, potential insurgency beating against containment, Eliot-style, in another poem. Barely held back, the slangy, pugnacious jazzman in "Shoot it Jimmy!" (XVII) declares:

Our orchestra
is the cat's nuts—

Banjo jazz
with a nickelplated

amplifier to
soothe

the savage beast— (CWP1, 216)

"*Our orchestra*," in epiglottal upthrust, may be "the cat's nuts," in slammed-down, hard-*t* avowal, but that is only a frustrated pull against the leash, as "*jazz*" tugs at "Ban*jo*," "am*p*lifier" at "nickel*p*lated," while this "savage beast" is distinctly not soothed. "Get the rhythm," he cries in frustration:

That sheet stuff
's a lot of cheese

Man
gimme the key

and lemme loose—
I make 'em crazy

with my harmonies—
Shoot it Jimmy

But while the other jazzman has yet to strike up, the poem's "*me*" can only shoot his boastful way via "*Jimmy*" and the elisions ("gi*mme*," "le*mme*") in a would-be crazy spate running from "sh*ee*t stuff" to "ch*ee*se" to "key" to "harmon*ies*." However, Williams compactly grasps the vehemence, cutting *s* away from its noun, with Moore-like dash, to make "s-a-lot-of" slide containably in its line, while his final stanzas (or vindicated "sheet stuff") declare:

Nobody
Nobody else

but me—
They can't copy it

—a last audacity whose exact standpoint is best suggested by considering how Williams's whole position might be interpreted.

If, with Michael North, "one assumes that the speaker of the poem is black" (though pushing toward more certainty of color than the text really suggests) then the white poet's "assertion of difference and originality" under a different skin might seem egotistic and contradictory: that is, if one goes as far as North in further assuming that Williams is here echoing the famous song of the black vaudeville artist Bert Williams, "Nobody." In doing so, according to North, Williams the poet disparages his source, just as he convicts "the entire black race of being nobody" in *In the American Grain*, where he mentions his namesake.[9] Yet like the indomitable "Nobody" in the poem, the people in the "Advent of the Slaves" chapter are not reduced to nullities at all. As becomes evident, when the ironic tone of Williams's prose is listened to, he is actually mimicking and subverting those who negate the reality of black Americans: "When they try to make their race an issue—it is nothing. In a chorus singing *Trovatore*, they are nothing. But"—as negation starts to be overturned by positiveness—"saying *nothing*, dancing *nothing*, 'NOBODY,' it is a quality," soon becoming, most definitely, a qualitative "SOMETHIN' . . . a solidity, a racial irreducible minimum, which gives them poise in a world where they have no authority."[10] To say, therefore, "Nobody / Nobody else // But *me*" in the stressed up-leap of "Shoot it Jimmy!" is to burst forth with the same un-negative insistence, without necessarily being tied to either white or black: a vaunt, in the rapped-out emphasis of "They can't *copy* it" that takes us beyond the ego, Williams's or otherwise, to the greater issue of authentic art and its surpassing of representational copying by detachment's vigorous partnering.

This, then, is not Williams in blackface, as seen by North, trying and failing to make another's language "serve as the basis for a new American unity,"[11] but the poet of stylistic disengagement keeping a deft parallel with fervent fact—the maker of recreations whose alacrity prevents them being sucked down into literalness, just as other poems exert a designer's pull-back from emotional absorption. Thus detachedly *not* copying a sensuous, hothouse abundance in *Spring and All*'s second poem, "The Pot of Flowers,"[12] Williams is able to proceed with the cool, imitative dexterity of the reconstructor. Lineal slices or "petals" of intensity are to be vocally enjoyed because he has broken them away from a luscious, top-to-bottom representation and put them together again in a flotational assembly:

> petals aslant darkened with mauve
>
> red where in whorls
> petal lays its glow upon petal
> round flamegreen throats
>
> petals radiant with transpiercing light (CWP1, 184)

While the word-segments stay visually separate in the page's spacious design, their voicings hover together in disciplined out-thrusts. So the taut push of "pet*als aslant*" is matched by the spurt of breath —"red *where* in *whorls*"— which makes the terseness of "petal" lay its glow "upon petal / round *flame*-green *th*roats," in enunciatory discrimination rather than gorgeous indulgence. More petals spring out, but their "transpiercing light" is

> contending
>   above
>
> the leaves
> reaching up their modest green

—as the petals strive away: not by being textually "above" those leaves in still-life realism, but staying at a slant from their upward-reaching equals in a luminous composition that ultimately fits into the tight-vowelled confine of a "pot's rim."

Yet the pleasures of overflow remain a temptation. Williams's prose after the poem declares: "The rock has split, the egg has hatched, the prismatically plumed bird of life has escaped from its cage"[13]—an opening-out of the spectrum that will soon bring him (after the "Prismatic Colour" of Moore's poem, and the "prismatic colors glistening" in Whitman's *Sea-Drift*) to the "prismatically colorful" Montezuma of *In the American Grain*. More temperately, though, his description of the way he wrote the Tenochtitlan chapter ("in big square paragraphs like Inca masonry . . . no plaster—just fitted boulders")[14] points back to the vocal tensing-together of separate pieces in his verse which Moore's example encouraged: her doing "without connectives,"[15] like a "primitive masonry, the units unglued."[16] His own ungluings and re-connections along a new track (also exemplified for him in Moore's "wiping soiled words or cutting them clean out . . . with no attachments")[17] let him try various ways of concentrating inside a small arena a potentially over-diffuse feeling for the larger, sensuous universe. So in "The Eyeglasses" (Poem X),

> The universality of things
> draws me toward the candy
> with melon flowers that open
>
> about the edge of refuse
> proclaiming without accent
> the quality of the farmer's
>
> shoulders and his daughter's
> accidental skin, so sweet
> with clover and the small
>
> yellow cinquefoil . . . (CWP1, 204)

From universality to particulars: what might be cloyingly over-delicious, as the voice runs on without stop, is held back from dominance by line-break discipline and the sharp stanza cuts of the visual design. Thus melon flowers "open" with a jolt "about the edge of refuse": trash and blooms joined together by the same keen-edged severance that blithely proclaims "without accent" (and with no distinction between the stanza-separated parts so newly connected) "the quality of the farmer's // shoulders" and his daughter's skin—fortuitously arrived at, and with no special privilege divorcing what is human from the clover and the cinquefoil. All are to be viewed by "eyeglasses" that, like Williams's geometry elsewhere, "see everything and remain / related to mathematics."

There is, however, a more concise way of grasping a universal coherence inside a smaller one. By his image of the world's held-together structure, conditional upon a tiny local cluster, Williams comes to his remarkable new linkage, born of disconnection, in his twenty-second poem:

> so much depends
> upon
>
> a red wheel
> barrow
>
> glazed with rain
> water
>
> beside the white
> chickens (CWP1, 224)

Symmetric fragmentation—"upon" singled out, like each second line in the following stanzas, as visually dependent *from* its predecessor's longer overhang—incites a vocal piecing-together. For "up*on*," when spoken, has the airborne upstress that gives emphatic lightness to each part of the solidity it touches: not "The Réd Wheélbărrŏw" (in Williams's pronunciation of the poem's later title)[18] but, in more equal, buoyant spread, a "réd—wheél—bárrŏw." These indeed, in the sound-defined spaces, are the "interstices for the light"[19] which Williams saw in Moore's verse between the edges of objects, but which only reemerge for the ear after speech, having made "glazed" so firmly a part of "barrow," separates out more balanced parts. So the sheen of

ráin wătĕr

matches the gleam of

whíte chíckĕns

in a grounded closeness that is also a spacious composition.

Here again is a designer's detachment. Yet "The Red Wheelbarrow," like other poems in *Spring and All*, has sprung out of human involvement: that is, if it is true that Williams wrote the poem after he had visited a seriously ill patient and turned away to look through the sickroom window at barrow and chickens.[20] In that respect, the verse can be considered a hidden partnering of wretchedness, just as "To An Old Jaundiced Woman" (XVI) is overt. When Williams cites Gaunt's attempt to console Bolingbroke in *Richard II* ("Suppose . . . thy steps" into banishment "no more / Than a delightful measure or a dance")[21] by describing it in the *Spring and All* prose as "a dance over the body of his condition accurately accompanying it,"[22] he suggests the springy steps that can only be close to misery by keeping a rhetorical distance.

O tongue
licking the sore on
her netherlip

O toppled belly

O passionate cotton
stuck with
matted hair (CWP1, 215)

The cry of apostrophic "O's" addresses physical ignominy, not the old woman herself. The uplifted voice of formal symmetry ("*t*ongue . . . *t*oppled") with its exalted, acoustic balance ("O passi*o*nate cott*o*n") deliberately separates the sufferer from all that would drag her down. Everything that would topple the higher note with a belly, a tongue's monotonous "*li*cking" of the "nether*li*p," and sweaty garment "matted" with hair, is undauntedly raised by the voice, stanza after stanza, with an unmeshing of the tangle which can even take in

elysian slobber
upon
the folded handkerchief

Six-syllabled neatness in "the folded handkerchief" balances its counterpart in the slither of "*elys*ian *slo*bber": a stanzaic insouciance separating the old woman from her degradations, just as the final layout extricates her distinctive voice from its surrounding abasements:

I can't die

—moaned the old
jaundiced woman
rolling her saffron eyeballs

I can't die
I can't die

The first "I can't die" may seem a forlorn wail; but though misery's facts tug at it in monotone stresses ("m*o*aned . . . *o*ld . . . r*o*lling") the next "*I*," following the space on the page, is implacably separate from "saffron *eye*balls" and physical circumstance. "I can't die"—repeated, and tautly faster thus—is then to be heard not as pathos but the unsurrendering, teeth-clenched assertion that finally declares, word distinct from word: "I—C-A-N-T—die."

One realizes anew the Moore-like importance of keeping "the units unglued." If "Piece by piece we must loosen what we want," as Williams says of words plucked from the European mass in *The Great American Novel* (with those words "plastered with muck out of the cities")[23] then, in "The Agonized Spires" (XIII), with its tenements built on Manhattan granite—

Crustaceous
wedge
of sweaty kitchens on
rock (CWP1, 211)

—he must work his spoken way, line by line, through the apparent inseparability of "Crust*ace*ous we*dg*e," as it clings to "sweaty kit*ch*ens," in order to reach the harder clarity of "rock." But this is an extrication from grim circumstance which, as in the Jaundiced Woman poem, takes on more agile form when, in "Death the Barber" (XIV), dexterous talk dances out of mortality's grip. Where the live barber has to be differentiated so definitely from the other kind, nothing macabre can daunt this sprightly impetus:

Of death
the barber
the barber

talked to me
cutting my
life with
sleep to trim my hair— (CWP1, 212)

With enjambed shock ("cutting my / life with / sleep") and the startlingly casual—

It's just
a moment
he said, we die
every night—

—the unamazed everydayness of hairdressing patter (a discourse "of the newest / ways to grow / hair on // bald death") is amazingly invigorated, just as humdrum chat and the "of" format ("of the quartz lamp // and of old men / with third sets of teeth") are recharged at the end when there comes, "all to the cue," the entry

of an old man
who said
at the door—
Sunshine today!

Williams's razor-edged accuracy is sudden and perfect—the instant verifying of daily delight ("today!") just as the barber's difference from, yet nearness to, his deathly double keeps the language of life clean-cut and distinctly itself.

Williams is indeed at his best in the collection when he maintains such superfine alertness. Therefore, on guard against emotional slackening of speech in "The Rose" (VII), he constantly renews love's embodiment in metal, porcelain, copper, or steel. Sharp-tipped, ahead of cliché, at "the edge of the petal," it must ever be on the point of re-expression. But vigilance is altogether less evident in the last poem of *Spring and All* when a wildflower expands, "rich / in savagery— // Arab / Indian / dark woman," with a reminder of the extremes, sensuous or the reverse, to which Williams is tempted. On the one hand, we remember, he has rejected any drowning in the senses by his portrayal of Elsie, the figure of "voluptuous water" with her "dash of Indian blood," yet on the other he so delights in wildflower "savagery" that he foreshadows his plunge in the opposite direction: toward the verbal overflow of *In The American Grain* that promotes Daniel Boone as the "great voluptuary"[24] against the niggardly Puritan tradition, and has him married to his American ground by "a lavish, primitive embrace in savage, wild beast and forest . . . voluptuous, passionate, possessive in that place which he opened."[25]

Nevertheless, when the more attentive poet of *Spring and All* speaks in the prose, an accuracy of feeling is not lost inside the woods of over-clamorous adjectives. Then he too takes the "fastidious pains"[26] which he ascribes to the French explorer Champlain over the siting and construction of a city in the chapter "The Founding of Quebec." While the foreigner waits on the St. Lawrence River for news from an approaching skiff, Williams finds a contained, native excitement,

> a world of pleasure in watching just that Frenchman, just
> Champlain, like no one else about him, watching, keeping
> the thing whole within him with almost a woman's tenderness
> —but such an energy for detail—a love of the exact detail—
> watching that little boat drawing nearer on that icy bay. This
> is the interest I see. It is this man. This—me; this American . . .[27]

Without "lavish, primitive embrace," but with a more exact love, "the thing whole" is kept together by the kind of care that appreciates Mengelberg, the Dutch orchestral conductor, whom the final Lincoln chapter likens to "a woman drawing to herself . . . the myriad points of sound."[28] Then, with a vertebrate rigor that clusters rather than sprawls, Williams the poet is

> watching
> just that Frenchman
> just Champlain
> watching—
> such an energy for detail
> a love of the exact detail—
> watching that little boat
> this man
> This—me
> this American

It is a way of entering native ground by means of outsiders (like Robitza and the English grandmother) which goes further in a later chapter, by using the language of another Frenchman, Père Sebastian Râsles. Here also is a firm edge to feeling, and more extraordinarily so in its non-sentimentality. For the missionary's "hallowed, tender light of . . . love"[29] toward the Abenaki Indians entails his swallowing their alien food *and* difficult language (the foreignness of the devouring enacted by the sound of epistolary French: "*loups marins . . . tripes des rocher, excréscences de bois*"),[30] but taken so far in its harsh, digestive versatility that Williams as translator of "ce hameau à manger" can exclaim that their enemies' village is "given" them "to be *eaten!*"[31] Even so, the sureness of a French-yet-Indian entry into the New World is no longer a possibility by the time of the later chapters. After the arrival of Franklin's business ethic and Hamilton's Federalism, Williams's narrative ventures into a tribal

America are becoming obsolescent. His invention of an Abenaki princess for Aaron Burr, and Sam Houston's uneasy excursions to Indian life, belong to a weakened line of feeling that the Poe chapter eradicates entirely. For there Poe the critic scourges literature's "nameless rapture over nature" or absorption in the "meaningless lump of the lush landscape,"[32] while he exemplifies for Williams an un-verbose "cold logic," quite separate, in language and method, from "the smear of common usage."[33]

After the more balanced detachments and engagements in the best verse of *Spring and All*, Williams's celebration of Poe's distanced style (his "standing off to SEE instead of forcing himself too close")[34] seems yet another exaggerated flight from physical submergence. It is like an extreme recompense for a temporarily lost sense of actual ground when Poe's spiritual aloofness as critic (his words able "to tell his soul")[35] serves Williams's desire to proclaim "a *new* locality" ("the first great burst through to expression of a re-awakened genius of *place*").[36] But while Poe also becomes the means by which Williams attacks *Waste Land* erudition (there being nothing "offensively 'learned'" about the use of other cultures' "tags" by a Poe who "could look at France, Spain, Greece, and NOT be impelled to copy")[37] it is Eliot who lets us temper Williams's grander claims. Without admitting to a knowledge of *In the American Grain*, he, in his 1953 lecture "American Literature and the American Language," tacitly questions the assumptions of a key Williams word that he does indeed know. "What is identifiably local about Poe? . . . His favourite settings [in the fiction] are imaginary romantic places": the "dream world" confections of the untraveled provincial whose real world was Baltimore, Richmond, and Philadelphia.[38] So speaks the dismissive cosmopolitan, who from his youth has been spellbound by the rhythms of Poe's verse, as Williams was definitely not ("in this his 'method' escaped him")[39] but who at least performs the task—as Williams does in his poetry, long before his fascination with Poe had ended[40]—of bringing the over-aloof back to earth.

Nevertheless, Williams's artistic re-descending and unexaggerated ascent still take their cue from Poe. For when the latter's 1843 review derides the "elaborate doggerel" of Thomas Ward, writing as "Flaccus" in his long poem *Passaic*,[41] Williams discovers Sam Patch, the celebrated leaper into the Falls. "Shout! trump of Fame," cries Flaccus,

> till thy brass lungs burst out!
> Shout! mortal tongues! deep-throated thunders, shout!
> For lo! electric *genius*, downward hurled,
> Has startled *Science*, and illumed the world![42]

"There might have been some science," remarks Poe, "in jumping *up*."[43] But for Williams in *Paterson I* the "Great Descender" truly prompts a defiance of gravity, after he has jumped into the flood and the roar of inarticulate

America. Though "Speech had failed him" in the inexpressible manner of "To Elsie," and "The word had been drained of its meaning" by a "great silence," Sam Patch, with his body "frozen in an ice-cake," belongs to a clarity of vocal purpose gradually emerging. Up goes the leap from the rhyme with "death"— "Stale as a whale's breath; breath, breath!"—as the voice rapidly jolts forward at each repetition:

> Only of late, late! begun to know, to
> know clearly (as through clear ice) whence
> I draw my breath or how to employ it
> clearly—if not well:
>
> Clearly!
> speaks the red-breast his behest. Clearly!
> clearly! (*Paterson*, 20)

Just as the striver out of aridity in *The Waste Land* upholds with moment-by-moment care the impulse that will lead to the water-song of the hermit-thrush, so Williams makes bird speech the summit of ever-sharpening realization—not just "to know" but (like "*late*" exasperatingly stressed after "late") "to / know *clearly*." Lucidity's acoustic definiteness may flag ("clearly—if not well") but as the background to the keen, new insistence of "Clearly!": the "red-breast" speaking his "behest" with the quick, close-rhymed tenacity by which Williams (like Champlain "watching . . . watching, keeping the thing whole within him") stays to

> watch, wrapt! one branch
> of the tree at the fall's edge, one
> mottled branch

—and not just any branch, but one distinctively "*mottled*" branch of a thick sycamore, swaying less "among the rest." In that calming, the voice's tempo changes as the branch moves

> slowly
> with giraffish awkwardness, slightly
> on a long axis, so slightly

—"so slightly" (it must be said with care) "as hardly to be noticed," yet, as Williams emphasizes in his 1947 recording,[44] "in it*self* the tempest."

All quivers therefore on a dynamic axis: the structured vigor in Williams's verse that extends into the multifarious and finds its clear, animal expression in the redbreast's song and a "giraffish awkwardness." So, by similar compulsion ("I must tell you") he works his adamant way through the syntactic impediments and foliage of "Young Sycamore" to the bare-branched, animal-like exactness of "two // eccentric knotted / twigs / bending forward / hornlike" ("forward / hornlike," in tightly pinched assonance) "at the top"—an act of vocally compressive zeal that has equally made a hybrid poetic creature out of chickens, rainwater, and a wheelbarrow. Indeed, whether by fauna, flora, or juxtaposed assembly, the speaking self in Williams has not only created an animality for verse but found a widening and transformation through it. For Eliot (the non-dead Possum of Pound's renaming) the animal sense suddenly waking the body—the bear dance shaking the protégé in "Portrait of a Lady," the tiger leaping at the moribund in "Gerontion," the nightingale cries of meta-morphosed Philomela beating at sedentary stasis in *The Waste Land*—can also be the quiet stirring ("A rat crept softly through the vegetation") which gradually leads to Ferdinand's vocal emboldenings. But where such grada-tions of animal identity are ways of escaping the limits of ego, circumstance, or personal affliction, as well as homing in upon a lost sense of ground and winning it back in re-utterance, Moore is the undoubted leader. If we saw Williams and Eliot more clearly through her interplay of form and speech in previous verse, it is now her poetry of the 1920s and 1930s, with its birds, beasts, fauna, or geology, which provides an even sharper perspective—not just to illuminate Eliot's man-beasts, or Williams's daring configurations, but to reveal the different forces here impelling the verse-creatures of all three poets into remarkable animation.

Five

The Animal Vernacular

"Poetry is an . . . unmistakable vernacular like the language of the animals."
MARIANNE MOORE, reviewing Wallace Stevens[1]

The preference is clear. Living in a culturally difficult terrain—a "grassless, linksless, languageless country" where "letters are written . . . in plain American which cats and dogs can read!" ("England," 1920)—Moore brings to her poetic bestiary the quality of the untamed and uncommon. Even when her animals belong to the land of her birth, they fly, run, leap, or stand still in unashamed foreignness. But these wild embodiments of the alien or the *other* also spring, we remember, from an essential restraint: a pull-back on outgoing energies by a sense of privacy and self-discipline that lets vocal individuality shoot forth all the more with unarrogant exactness. It is a drama of keen opposites so crucial to her "foreign" progress as a poet of animality in the twenties that it takes on special significance when she comes to revise earlier work—not blunting the edges, as the older poet might do in perpetual changes of mind, but bringing to light the potential acuity lost inside the original version of a poem.

Notably she changed altogether the submissive and defeatist tenor of verse originally entitled "In Einar Jonsson's 'Cow'" (1915). She may elsewhere have balked at the constraints of a lifelong domesticity shared with her mother, as John Slatin observes,[2] but here she offers no rebellion. Having seen photographs of an Icelandic sculptor's work, based on Norse creation myths—the statue of the giant Ymir, lying on his back, suckling the cow Auðumbla, and "The Wave of the Ages," an upthrust of curving stone with a woman's head and body—she sets vertical aspiration alongside horizontal acquiescence, but not as a clash of contraries:

> Here we have thirst,
> And patience from the first,
>   And art—as in a wave held up for us to see—
>   In its essential perpendicularity: (qtd. in Willis, 9)

Whatever the "thirst" for greater things amongst such patient endurance, Moore's image of upsoaring "art" remains conspicuously narrow and static—a wave only just slightly unfrozen in stanza two, where it is said to be "Not chilly but / Intense." Indeed, with no "variation of the perpendicular" or spectrum-like abundance envisaged by her 1919 poem "In the Days of Prismatic Colour," the "held up" art is here made to bend down in Ymir-like supineness: "The spectrum's cut / Out of the body of the world, laid on its back, / And made subordinate." Ending the poem, Moore may let in a hint of irony, "We recognize no lack," but it would need her later changes—a 1921 revision of the second stanza and the re-titling of poem as "An Egyptian Pulled Bottle in the Shape of a Fish" (*Observations*)—to show what she had kept out of the verse: a defiant spirit played against excess humility, together with the whole resurgent spread of art's gleaming possibilities. Now they come through with a significant change of animal and foreign country, as an Icelandic cow gives way to a glass fish recently discovered in Egypt:

> Not brittle but
> Intense—the spectrum, that
>> Spectacular and nimble animal the fish
>> Whose scales turn aside the sun's sword with their polish. (OB, 20)

"Intense—" at last earns its keep, speedily carrying the eye to the new brilliances demanding adroit separations of sound, as "*spec*trum" expands to the radiance of "*Spec*tacular," and "*nimble*" is deftly differentiated from "a*nimal*." It is this "fi*sh*" (as *sh* slips into a more agile *s*-form) "Whose scales turn a*side*" (and acoustically deflect "a*side*") "the sun's *sword*": all with the "polish" of an inner secrecy kept safe as it adventurously matches the world's glare.

Rising out of Moore's natural restraint and domestic limits, the same creaturely toughness is asserted—but with the confines of home suggestively enlarged to become a place of un-timorous occupation—in "The Frigate Pelican" (1934). "*This* one" most distinctively—the Caribbean fish-seizing bird, not to be confused with the "stalwart swan" ferrying Hansel and Gretel home in the Grimms' fairy tale, or a "less limber animal" of safer comforts—

> This one
> finds sticks for the swan's-down-dress
> of his child to rest upon and would
>> not know Gretel from Hänsel.
>> As impassioned Händel—
>
> meant for a lawyer and a masculine German domestic
> career—clandestinely studied the harpsichord
> and never was known to have fallen in love,
>> the unconfiding frigate-bird hides
> in the height and in the majestic
> display of his art . . . (PMM, 204)

If the hurts and awkwardness of American ground are the essential basis for making it a place to reside in, the bird has no qualms about creating a nest out of sharp edges. Hence the "*sticks*" on which the young's soft "*swan's-down-dress*" must, with an acoustic hardening of the bed, "*rest* upon"; the further indifference ("*Gretel*" played with greater hardness against "*rest*") of a bird who "would / not know Gretel from Hänsel"; and, set against the softer "Hänsel," the extra-hard *d* determination of "impassioned Han*d*el," as "Han*d*el . . . clandestinely studied the harpsichord" ("*st*udied" with the tight concentration begot of "clande*st*inely"). It is a passionateness breaking from cover, only to stay concealed when the "unconfi*d*ing frigate-bird hi*d*es" like Handel, but (with breath's aspirate outstretch) "hi*d*es / in the *height* and in the majestic / display of"—soaring with an unaspirated thrust—"his *art*."

Again we glimpse the well-hidden Moore herself: not as an ego projected into the animal, but as a poet refusing to temper the art's animalesque force. But in creating a huge poetic menagerie and reaching beyond her own marked sense of constraint and drudgeries, she avoids any pose of invulnerability, as when she boasts in an earlier poem that "With an elephant to ride upon . . . she shall outdistance calamity anywhere she goes" ("Diligence is to Magic as Progress is to Flight," 1915). That is the kind of feigned insouciance, however, which casts a light on the way that Eliot similarly puts round himself, through greater strain, a different animal armor—a fantasy version of invulnerability which is the potent beast-man of the 1918 "Sweeney among the Nightingales." If Eliot is reacting in the poem to the sexual humiliation he suffered through his first wife's adulterous liaison with Bertrand Russell, as Ronald Schuchard suggests,[3] then "Apeneck Sweeney" is an insensate answer to pain. As he lounges in a brothel, indifferent to all treachery, ancient and modern (with the murdered Agamemnon crying out from the poem's Greek epigraph) he

> spreads his knees
> Letting his arms hang down to laugh,
> The zebra stripes along his jaw
> Swelling to maculate giraffe (CPP, 56)

The laughter may be as forced as the jerky trochees and assonance: "Ápenĕck Swéenĕy" spreading his "*knees*" so wide that a comic fall awaits "The person in the Spanish cape" who soon tries to sit on them. But even the protean escape from a fixed, mockable position or defilement ("*Letting*" dangled out into "*laugh*"; the "zebra stripes . . . Swelling" to the giraffe's stainless spots) expresses, as much as Moore's beasts, when she is *not* pretending to be nonchalant about calamity, an uncrushable inviolateness. It persists behind Sweeney's evolutionary jumps, stanza by stanza, when "The silent man in mocha brown" who "Sprawls and gapes" is changed to the "silent vertebrate" of firmer backbone, who then becomes a vegetation god ("Branches of wistaria / Circumscribe a golden grin") before he takes wing. Metamorphosed from the lower animals to the higher, he who spans the ages is equally one with the

"nightingales . . . singing near / The Convent of the Sacred Heart" and those
in the Colonus grove where a murdered cuckold, not just Christ, has been
sacrificed. So "they sang within the bloody wood / When Agamemnon cried
aloud" ("al*oud*" dissonantly jarring against "*wood*"),

> And let their liquid siftings fall
> To stain the stiff dishonoured shroud.

Thus, with Sweeney's laugh bitterly let fall, down comes the bird slime of thud-
ding iambics, "Tŏ stáin—thĕ stiff—dĭshón—ouřed" (and *loud*ly shameful)
"sh*roud*."

Whatever the vengeful noise, Eliot is moving toward the "inviolable voice"
of Philomela, transformed into a nightingale; and in that one has the clue to
the greater poetic outcome of his undaunted animal sense. For when a different beast-man hits at pretensions rather than sexual malefactors in the 1915
"Mr. Apollinax" (starring Bertrand Russell as a professorial satyr rather than
adulterous threat) the comedy's proteanism more clearly heralds the stretching
of verse-skin and identity in *The Waste Land*. As this foreign man-animal-god
shakes a staid American scene with his "dry and passionate talk," to "the beat
of centaur's hoofs," he resounds with subversive change. "In the pal*ace* of Mrs.
Phl*accus*" (with its stately-absurd chime) "at Professor Channing-Cheetah's,"
he "laughed" (as laughs the forthcoming outrageous rhyme with "Che*etah's*")[4]
"like an irresponsible *foetus*." What was comic ferocity in the Sweeney poem is
here the sinister merriment of perpetual change, "submarine and profound,"
as the unborn child gives way to predatory age, with its laughter

> Like the old man of the sea's
> Hidden under coral islands
> Where worried bodies of drowned men drift down in the green silence,
> Dropping from fingers of surf. (CPP, 31)

As the "prof*ound*" laughter dies away, and the "worried bodies" of his hosts
are dragged out of their intellectual depth, drifting "d*own*" mellifluously "in
the green silence" of semi-romantic lingering, those "fingers" become an instant reminder of the shape-shifter's body. Abandoning sea-drift, "I looked
for the head of Mr. Apollinax rolling under a chair // Or"—the head severed
by the stanza-cut, only to reappear, with lingered mockery—"grinning over a
screen."

The protean creature's freedom continues, born from the same authorial
need that keeps the ever-changing Sweeney safe from tragedy's pain. But if the
animals of Moore's verse imaginatively rise out of different emotional constraints and show Eliot's man-beasts fantastically boundless by comparison,
Eliot's satire, in its turn, shows up the fast-moving vocal creature that Williams
brings to life with more satiric joyousness. For while Apollinax drowns emi-

nent Bostonians "under coral islands," Williams, in his own cultural comedy of America, "It is a Living Coral" (1923), overturns the official academy art of an "island in the sea," the nation's Capitol, with a multiplicity of wilder native energies. In a building "archaically fettered / to produce // *E Pluribus Unum*," where Constantino Brumidi's frescoes in the rotunda set Mercury, god of commerce, next to Robert Morris, financier of the Revolution, and Minerva, goddess of wisdom and arts, by the side of generators and inventors—and where the plates of the Capitol's dome expand and contract—the stanzas puff out and squeeze back in Williams's own impish creation of One from the Many:

Commerce Minerva
Thomas

Jefferson John Hancock
at

the table . . . (CWP1, 255)

With an unpunctuated slide of names, the list defies one's speaking it slowly. For speed, as in Williams's 1945 recording,[5] fuses the crammed pieces to make the hilarious new body of an American counter-art:

It climbs
it runs, it is Geo.
Shoup

of Idaho, it wears
a beard

it fetches naked
Indian

women from a river

"It . . . it . . . it . . . it . . . it." One after the other, the nonstop voice holds together the multi-limbed parts of the amazing art-animal that not only "climbs" and "runs" but unleashes George Shoup from his abbreviated inscription and senatorial sobriety in the Capitol's Statuary Hall.[6] Instantly turning into the bearded Apollinax-style satyr who fetches those naked Indian women (all a further Williams invention) he belongs to the rapidity which also rams into one indigenous whole another senator, a chief justice, an explorer, and pioneers: "Banks White Columbus / stretched // in bed men felling trees." Nor can the Honorable Michael C. Kerr be stopped from losing his solemnity as "one-time / Speaker of / the House // of Representatives" when the unhalted voice makes him share the crush of a "rowboat" with *Perry* (so small a name after the unfurling of "*Representatives*"). But here, with Admiral Perry, Williams's multi-personed composite has become his most dissident retort to Capitol art. William Powell's painting "The Battle of Lake Erie," commemorating the American victory over the British in 1813, pictures the epauletted Commodore at the moment when he has abandoned his disabled flagship for another vessel. Staunchly upright in his boat, he points the way to helmsman and rowers, while flotsam and a corpse are left behind. In Williams's re-grouping, however (one's fast-speaking pressure unslackened to the poem's end) it is

> Perry
> in a rowboat on Lake
> Erie
>
> changing ships the
> dead
>
> among the wreckage
> sickly green

—a cascade of the "scaleless // jumble" that Williams saw earlier in the Capitol pictures: "the / *dead*" emphatically sounded into prominence as they cut against the Commodore's progress, while wreckage blocks the route of heroic art's certainties.

It is the irreverent upset which also sharpens one's sense of a very different attitude in Moore's poem "The Hero" (1932). For whereas Williams delivers his ripostes by jamming separate pieces together as new art-composites—new animals, in fact—Moore, the celebrant of a bird who "hides / in the height and in the majestic / display of his art," makes her visit to another national monument the occasion for celebrating, with her own eye for separatenesses joined, a height of achievement which at the same moment remains hidden and secret. Not to be penetrated by the glances of the sightseeing tourist, the Washington statuary at Mount Vernon shines for her with a moral power that comes from within—a sculptured art "not out / seeing a sight" but, in flashing reversal and the infinitive's special emphasis, "the rock-crystal thing to see": vision made acoustically sharp as "*crystal*" leaps to "*start*ling" and the hero-rock becomes "the startling El Greco / brimming with inner light" (PMM, 187). But for Williams, just as revealingly, Washington in *In the American Grain* is a "keeper of the stillness within himself,"[7] not because of any spiritual virtue but because of his nearly ungovernable rages. It is also the energy of Washington as compositional improviser, not moral hero, which has special appeal for a self-identifying Williams in the 1935 libretto *The First President*. With an echo from Moore's "Poetry" about "imaginary gardens with real toads in them," Washington is the man who created "an imaginary republic" and defended it with "a very real army."[8] Since "It was a country he pasted together—a good deal out of shoddy—to represent the thing we still labor to perfect,"[9] there is special affinity for a poet who himself fashions the fortuitous and unpromising into a new coherence.

It is appropriate, therefore, that Williams, castigator of those who copy other nations' art, should then proceed in a 1938 poem to cluster out of fragments an essentially native entirety in sound and sight—no "rock-crystal thing" but a newly made object gleaming with its own particular light:

Between Walls
the back wings
of the

hospital where
nothing

will grow lie
cinders

in which shine
the broken

pieces of a green
bottle (CWP1, 453)

Moore-like regulation is not to be forgotten: the holding-back in order to let go more surely. Thus, syntactically cramped, impeded by title and hospital wings in terse abutment, delayed by a clause, and starved of a verb, the sentence only releases its stored-up force when it can be said at last, with extra definiteness, that "*nothing //* will grow." For "*nothing*" after "*wings*" sets free the small, insistent glow of "*cinders*"—those "in which sh*i*ne," brightened by "*lie*," the regathered parts of a new, balanced order:

 the broken pieces
   of
  a green bottle

When Williams drafted this earlier, he wrote "in which // shine pieces" and left out "broken."[10] Inserted now, however, its key, vocal function suddenly becomes clear as it wakes up fellow-plosives in "*pieces*" and "*bottle*": everything, in fact, which not only pieces together afresh one "green bottle" but yields from this desert of American ground its unforeseen verdure.

By the same impulse, he rears out of the industrial setting of "Classic Scene" (1937) a more massive object, elementally nonhuman but with a human significance:

A power-house

in the shape of
a red brick chair
90 feet high (CWP1, 444)

Saying the first stanza, one is also keeping it erect. For the abrupt stops ("house," "chair," "high") after each section of the verbless sentence are the taut means to maintain the vertebrate stance of the giants who occupy such out-of-doors furniture. Thus, unsaggingly, "on the seat" of the chair,

sit the figures
of two metal
stacks—aluminum—

commanding an area
of squalid shacks—
side by side—

With "two metal / stacks" kept acoustically upright by the abrupt insertion of "al—oo—minum," the lip-pressed sound of "aluminum" impels "command-ing an area / of squalid shacks" to become a large, compositional grasp of those shacks, "side by side," rather than an expression of dominance. Those who sit with *their* unslackened dignity inside the houses of the poor have their outer manifestation in the huge chair and figures of the power plant—the re-straint which indeed has its own kind of power when the spoken poem allows a final release of breath that is no more impetuous than the plant with its emis-sions. Out of one stack,

buff smoke
streams while under
a grey sky
the other remains

—with text-reading surprise after the stanza-gap—

passive today—

Being thus emphatically *"passive"* and not having to insist on outward show, the command is all the surer, as Williams maintains the erect verse-posture of the newly made thing.

But where he defends such holding power as a vital capaciousness, the body is more obviously not an object but a caged, defiant beast. This, "Ladies and gentlemen!" as the fairground barker raucously proclaims at the start of "The Sea-Elephant" (1930), is "the greatest / sea-monster ever exhibited / alive"—"al-i-i-ve" with the syllable-opening reverberance that also enunciates, through the narrator's voice, the gaping appetite of the Poetry Monster: "O *wallow /*

of flesh *where* / are // there fish enough . . . ?" Heard on its own, it roars with insatiableness:

> Blouaugh! (feed
> me) my
> flesh is riven—

—a ravenous snort ("Blwaah!" in Williams's 1952 reading at Princeton),[11] whose bracketed translation is made to look pusillanimously pedantic by being stretched across the stanza-gap. Yet cramped or bulged, the uneven-looking stanzas reflect the body of the monster, pinched in one place by torments and impertinences, only to extrude elsewhere:

> the
> troubled eyes—torn
> from the sea
> (In
>
> a practical voice) they
> ought
> to put it back where
> it came from (CWP1, 341)

If one follows Williams's recording, one can act out the supercilious "practical voice" in the manner of a genteel lady flinching from poetry's rougher vitality. But whatever the style adopted, the monster's retort to its patronizers is clearly thunderous. Rising "bearded / to the surface," it erupts with a "Blouaugh!" that pits itself against the poetasters' circus:

> Swing—ride
> walk
> on wires—toss balls
> stoop and
>
> contort yourselves—
> But I
> am love. I am
> from the sea—

Suddenly firm amidst the commotion, the creature's even-stressed insistence, "Í—am—lóve" speaks ultimately for the balance struck by Williams's art. Just as passionate defiance ("Blouaugh!") stays roaringly undiffuse through form's counter-cuts, so capacious love for the world's bounty stays unflaccidly tight: caged by form (that disciplined side of Williams) yet (his other side) bursting free with indomitable exactness.

Moore heard Williams deliver the poem at a Brooklyn reading in 1936 and was exhilarated by the occasion. But though she told him that she and her companion at the reading, Elizabeth Bishop, were "animals with a little different markings from yours,"[12] her own "animal" quality stems, like his, from competing elements in her own nature. Against the unconquerably fierce strives an equally moderating force, though in ways that could weaken the counterpoint of opposites. It is, for instance, her attempt to reconcile the "wild and gentle" in "Sea Unicorns and Land Unicorns" (1924) that subjugates "this haughtiest of beasts," when the American unicorn is "tamed only by a lady," the Virgin Queen, "inoffensive like itself" (OB, 91). But when delight in an animal's self-restraint rides in tension with a sense of its untamed power, Moore shuns docility as much as does Williams's sea-elephant. She may not, like him, blast the ear of a fastidious lady, but hers is the tart voice which warns those who toy with a sleeping cat in the poem "Peter" (the syllabic paragraph version of 1919 in *Observations*)[13] that they face imminent retaliation:

> Demonstrate
> on him how
> the lady caught the dangerous southern snake, placing a
> forked stick on either
> side of its innocuous neck; one need not try to stir
> him up; his prune shaped head and alligator's eyes are
> not a party to the
> joke . . . (OB, 51)

"Demonstrate on *him*"—if you dare—the risky catching of the snake by the finicky neatness of placing "a forked stick on either / side of its innocuous neck." As emphasis acerbically cautions, "one need not try to stir / him up": he whose "alligator's eyes" (have you observed?) are distinctly "*not* / a party to the / joke" (if that's what you think it).

Set to a different scale, however, the eruptive potential of the animal and its constraint have their greatest expression in the opposites that play against each other in Moore's 1923 "An Octopus" (*The Dial* version, December 1924). Here Mount Rainier's master-creature, the glacier, accommodates quiescence and sudden force, sensitivity and danger's delight, the guilefully hidden and the joyously exposed, the guardedly remote and the openly revealed. In the spirit of contrariety touching the mountain's many animals, trees, flowers, and rocks, what at the beginning is "Deceptively reserved and flat"—a page-flat metaphor halted in a sibilant hiss:

> *An Octopus*
> of ice.

—is soon on the move with factual, hammering *f*s ("twenty-eight ice *f*ields *f*rom *f*ifty to *f*ive hundred *f*eet") that, in a dexterous shift of mouth and tongue, are that many "*f*eet *th*ick": a "*th*i*ck*" ice, however, with "unimagined de*l*i*c*acy":

> "Picking periwinkles from the cracks"
> or killing prey with the concentric crushing rigor of the python,
> it hovers forward "spider fashion
> on its arms" misleadingly like lace;
> its "ghostly pallor changing to the metallic tinge of an anemone-starred pool."
>   (OB, 83)

While quoted or unquoted segments from Moore's magazine reading hit the eye in their recalcitrant separateness, it is the imperturbable, onward-moving voice which holds the facets together as one extraordinary beast. With meticulous de*l*i*c*acy and *p*-deft care ("*P*i*c*king *p*eriwin*k*les from the cra*ck*s") it turns the hard *c*'s brutal ("*k*illing . . . with . . . *c*oncentric *c*rushing rigor"), yet changes the terrible ice-python to a tentative spider, "misleadingly like lace"— though "mislead*ing*ly" a preparation for the unexpectedness of ice's "ghostly pallor chang*ing*" from the phantasmal to the hard-edged color of "the green metallic ting*e*."

By a further misleading (though for the moment without the overt presence of the octopus-glacier in the poem) any over-humanized way of seeing, like the lake "in the shape of the left human foot, / which prejudices you in favor of itself," finds itself deceived. For the heaping-up of rock treasure—"calcium gems and alabaster pillars, / topaz, tourmaline crystals and amethyst quartz": all painstakingly amassed and vocally shouldered as an increasing burden of words—is not, after all, leading to the palatial home of the mountain bears. In fact their den, teasingly, is somewhere else, "concealed in the confusion" (more expensiveness dismissively scattered) "of 'blue forests thrown together with marble and jasper and agate / as if whole quarries had been dynamited'"—an imaginary explosion and the verse-line's lengthy strewing that bring into spoken view a more truly valuable "fragment":

> And farther up, in stag-at-bay position
> as a scintillating fragment of these terrible stalagmites,
> stands the goat,
> its eye fixed on the waterfall which never seems to fall—
> an endless skein swayed by the wind,
> immune to force of gravity in the perspective of the peaks.

With the Landseer "*stag*-at-bay position" toughened as a "*f*ra*g*ment of these terrible *stal*a*g*mites," there "*st*ands" all the firmer the short-line standpoint of "the goat" on syntax's hard crag. Unshakenly fixed, it sees across a stretch of lineal space "the waterfall which"—far above the Adamic kind—"never seems to fall."

So at that point Moore stays aloft on the mountain with un-didactic moral acuity. She does not have to struggle like Eliot toward the sound of hermit-thrush and cock on the various heights of "What the Thunder Said," but she does need the same undefeated stamina that brings her to the goat's visionary successors, "the eleven eagles of the west." Tourist chatter about them ("They make a nice appearance, don't they, / happy seeing nothing?") accentuates, beyond such a question, the birds' sharper sight and hearing:

> Perched on treacherous lava and pumice—
> those unadjusted chimney-pots and cleavers
> which stipulate "names and addresses of persons to notify
> in case of disaster"—
> they hear the roar of ice and supervise the water
> winding slowly through the cliffs

In a sentence broken into by satirized over-humanizing—the pedantic-squeamish mentality which decries the rocks' "unadjusted" disorder and razor edges, while stipulating rules "in case of disaster"—the eagles' fearless poise becomes all the stronger. "Perched" on volcanic ground (with the voice lifted on "pumice" to let in the legalistic interruption, before resuming the sentence in accrued intentness) the disaster-indifferent birds adhere to nature's sterner law. They "hear the roar of ice" and, with a *vision* implicit in "super*vise*," seemingly govern by sight "the water / winding": as far removed from the tourists' view of them ("happy seeing nothing?") as from the Greeks (the ethical idlers of the poem, "Like happy souls in hell") and the National Park's attempted regulation of disobedient Adam in "this game preserve / where 'guns, nets, seines, traps, and explosives, / hired vehicles, gambling, and intoxicants are prohibited.'"

It is the articulation of a fiercer law—Moore's anger launched with control against other offenders—that ultimately begets, with ice-clear sharpness, the return of the central creature, the octopus. By hard-edged vocal incisions ("con*tact* ... in*tact* ... *cut* ... sacrosan*ct*," like "de*cor*um" soon after) Moore goes from the image of the mountain—

> this fossil flower concise without a shiver,
> intact when it is cut,
> damned for its sacrosanct remoteness—

—to Henry James—

> "damned by the public for decorum";
> not decorum but restraint

—as she swiftly rewords the scorned "decorum." *Her* "restraint" is audible in the measured intensity by which she tartly makes clear (James's art and her own equally defended) that

> it is the love of doing hard things
> that rebuffed and wore them out—a public out of sympathy with neatness.
> Neatness of finish!

—the phrase, originating from Williams and Ruskin,[14] hardly uttered in grim derision before it is repeated on a higher note of indignation: "Neatness of FINISH!" Against that, "Relentless accuracy"—"*accuracy*," to be vehemently precise—

> is the nature of this octopus
> with its capacity for fact.

—"*accuracy*" heard in the "*fact*" of this "*octopus*" with a devouring power that equals Williams's sea-elephant as it shears twigs, twists trees, and makes branches into "flattened mats." At the last, on the planed, polished mountain and with the poem's fast-growing impetus ("lightning flashing . . . rain falling . . . snow falling") it makes its appearance as

> the glassy octopus symmetrically pointed,
> its claw cut by the avalanche
> "with a sound like the crack of a rifle,
> in a curtain of powdered snow launched like a waterfall."

So, to a rifle-crack sound, National Park regulations are disobeyed by nature, and a prelapsarian vision rules in the launch and suspense of the avalanche: that further "waterfall which never seems to fall."

Moore's last lines still seem to ring in Williams's ears when he finds it astounding that "so slight a woman can so roar, like a secret Niagara."[15] His own Niagara, by contrast, in "Paterson: the Falls" (1943) lets out the "disembodied roar!" which leads him via the Passaic to the mythic giantism of the postwar *Paterson*. There, on the female Garret Mountain, as opposed to the male city, Mount Rainier's bears, goat, chipmunk, ptarmigan, marmot, eagles, ponies and glacier-octopus have their counterparts in real, imaginary, or hybrid animals. But by contrast with the unmythic Moore—and a token of the ambitions that take Williams away from short-line factuality—his beasts spring into life less as independent beings than as explicit offshoots of the creative mind. Since "without invention" in *Paterson II*, "the small footprints / of the mice will not appear," it is consistent that Paterson's climbing of the mountain should beget the "grasshopper of red basalt" tumbling "from the core of his mind" or the scampering of a chipmunk when "the mind grows, up flinty pinnacles." Imagination goes further at the summit where Italian-American picnickers are cast in the ancient light of Pan, goat-men, and animal-human lusts—a dancer's leg raised with "the / bovine touch! The leer, the cave of it, / the female of it" (in that excitedly built-up "*female*" emphasis) "facing the male, the satyr—(Priapus!)." It is the satyric "core of gaiety" that looks forward to the moment in *Paterson V* (1958) when tragedy is out-laughed with animal versatility. What in "The Sea-Elephant" was an exactly aimed defiance ("Í—aḿ—lóve") becomes the assertive spread by which the century's horrors are matched by art's enduring power: "I saw love / mounted naked on a horse / on a swan / the tail of a fish / the bloodthirsty conger eel . . ."

But such "love," though strenuously upheld at each triadic line-end, is no longer the accurately focused delight which brings together a new body, a felt animality, out of juxtaposed pieces. Nor does it have the upreared sureness that comes from embroilment in solidities—the descending-ascending motion remembered by his call in *Paterson II* to go down "fearlessly— / to . . . the screaming dregs" and "From that base, unabashed, to regain / the sun kissed summits of love!" Even at a distance from his surer impulses in *Paterson III*, where he echoes Eliot's pattern ("to start again") in *Four Quartets*,[16] he still displays, if self-consciously ("to begin, to begin again"), the instinctive need to win his shapes by descent into the shapeless: "Go down, peer among the fishes."

One notices, however, that he has already achieved such an aim, without advertisement, in the textual compression and acoustics of "The Cod-Head" (1932):

Miscellaneous weed
strands, stems, debris—
firmament

to fishes—
where the yellow feet
of gulls dabble—

oars whip
ships churn to bubbles— (CWP1, 357)

All is surface disarray in the vocal thrusts of individual words and lines: "strands" jarred hard against "weed"; "stems" played off "strands"; and "firmament" (surprise companion for unheavenly "debris") an equally incongruous partner as "*fir*mament // to *fi*shes." But the squeeze of the tiny stanza lets Williams grip the brokenly haphazard together in a controlled cacophony, overlaying "*fi*shes" with gulls' "*feet*" and plosively striking at their casual "da*bb*le" with "oars whi*p*"—the short-line burst where words, not just "shi*ps*" after "wh*ip*," churn the remembrance of "da*bble*" into a chaos of "bu*bble*s." The text-reading eye also sees underwater breakage: the split of "waver-" from "ing" in refractive shimmer; the sudden dash which cuts sight off at "through which—"; a "cod- // head" severed across stanzas. Yet stanzaic brevity equally ensures that the pulse of a gathering cohesion begins to be heard:

> amorphous waver-
> ing rocks—three fathom
> the vitreous
>
> body through which—
> small scudding fish deep
> down—and
>
> now . . .

After the poem's initial short stabs, lengthened phrasing allows the basis of a rhythm to emerge. The voice which pauses on the upnote of "which—" and then descends with "small s*cudd*ing fish deep / *down*," prepares the ear "*now*" for "a l*ull*ing lift / and f*all*":

> now a lulling lift
> and fall—
> red stars—a severed cod-
>
> head between two
> green stones—lifting
> falling

So, all this while, the voice which clashed random fragments together at the start has been searching for a deeper conjunction: the up-down beat, by which the severed head, visually floating between stanzas, is tightly part (wedged in sound "bet*ween* two / *green* stones") of the greater "vitreous / body" to which all the scattered pieces now belong.

Without *Paterson*-type proclamations, it is the firm shape and rhythm of non-human energy, or animal power beyond the personal ego, which Williams re-elicits in "The Term" (1937). What sounds like drift (a sheet of brown paper "about the length // and apparent bulk / of a man . . . rolling with the // wind slowly over / and over in / the street") is suddenly tautened for the ear by small stanzas as

> a car drove down
> upon it and
> crushed it to
>
> the ground . . . (CWP1, 451)

With "drove down" a harsh impress changes "over and over" from looseness to resilience—a flattening "down" on that "ground" which finds its tough obverse in "Unlike" as the voice's emphatic upturn plays against "crushed":

> Unlike
> a man it rose
> again rolling
>
> with the wind over
> and over to be as
> it was before

Channeled tightly now, the wind pulse driving the sheet of paper is voiced with the new, insistent regularity—"rose / again rolling"; "over / and over"—which makes constancy ride change so definitely: "to be" (with syllabic weight now shifting) "as it was before." It is the small, local conduit for the universal—"so much depends / upon . . ."—which has its notable counterparts in Williams's 1938 poem "The Poor." The force suggested by the little inlets of a thrifty people's art (panels of a house's cast-iron balcony "showing oak branches in full leaf") is finally unleashed at full spate when an old man is seen sweeping "his own ten feet" of sidewalk

> in a wind that fitfully
> turning his corner has

—with amazing onslaught at the turn of the line-end corner—

> overwhelmed the entire city

Yet all is forecast by Williams's opening words ("It's the anarchy of poverty / delights me"): a clear echo, as Vivienne Koch observed,[17] of Moore in "The Steeple-Jack" (1932) where "it is a privilege to see so / much confusion," but said with a cooler voice. For her confusion-accepting gusto, also directed at a specially American scene, contains the realization that she must come at it from a distance, with a foreigner's detachment, an animal zest, and a scrupulous care before the place can be inhabited by the sensibility. Alien eyes therefore lead back to homegrown dexterities when Moore's original version of "The Student," first published alongside "The Steeple-Jack," invokes the French-born painter of American wildlife: "When Audubon adopted us he taught / us how to dance."[18] In the 1932 version of "The Steeple-Jack" in *Poetry*, however, a German painter teaches from the start an unshockable agility; for "*Dürer*" (only he, one must emphasize, and no East Coast native)

> would have seen a reason for living
> in a town like this, with eight stranded whales

to look at; with the sweet sea air coming into your house
on a fine day . . .

This is not like Moore speaking later in "A Carriage from Sweden" (1939) about
a foreign artifact, now in a Brooklyn museum: "They say there is a sweeter
air / where it was made than we have here." Instead, "The Steeple-Jack" ro-
bustly embraces what is native and in front of you: "the sweet sea air coming
into your house" and not to be divorced from the equal attraction—all in the
speaker's imperturbable tone of complete reasonableness—of the whale's disaster. Urged on by the voice of non-amazement, "You" must blithely accept
not just Dürer's "reason" for taking up residence here (the stranded whales on
Long Island or Brooklyn supplying what he missed off the Dutch coast)[19] but
the Düreresque discipline that ties it to "water etched / with waves as formal
as the scales / on a fish." Indeed, without demurral, "You" are being educated
by Moore to move between the contraries of wildness and order, as human
formality interchanges with the nonhuman—animal nature regulating the
man-made and vice versa. So the insouciant voice beats out "One by one, in
two's, in three's" the tick-tock of seagulls flying over the town clock, who also

> flock
> mewing where
>
> a sea the purple of the peacock's neck is
>   paled to greenish azure as Dürer changed
> the pine green of the Tyrol to peacock blue and guinea
> grey. You can see a twenty-five-
>   pound lobster and fish nets arranged
> to dry . . .

Where the different purposes crisscross with a shock—the sea's paling to
"greenish azure" and the painter's changing the "pine green" of the hill in
his 1490s watercolor for the needs of perspective[20]—"You" accept everything
through a vocal hardiness of color-change that plosively strides, with animal
certainty, from "the *purple* of the *peacock's neck* . . . *paled to greenish azure*"
and thence bears up the heavier, factual weight of "a twenty-five- / pound lob-
ster and fish nets." With these "arranged / to dry" by artist-like ordering, there
enters the regimented sound of nature's own wild, compressive formalism,
"The // whirlwind fifeanddrum of the storm."

Yet as the wind "disturbs stars in the sky and the / star on the steeple,"
the terms on which Moore accepts such orderly disorder—the moral basis for
dwelling in this place—must be more exactly defined. The vocal aplomb that
regards it as "privilege to see so much confusion" and that welcomes in stanza
five the profusion of transplanted, alien flora ("the tropics at first hand: the
trumpet-vine, / fox-glove, giant snap-dragon," and many more) is rigorously

cut back in stanzas six and seven. "The climate // is not right," in emphatic curtness,

> for the banyan, frangipan, the
> jack-fruit tree; nor for exotic serpent
> life. Ring lizard and snake-skin for the foot if you see fit,
> but here they've cats not cobras
> to keep down the rats.

No place here, then, for unsuitable flora or the snake of the Fall and the temptations of opulence. "Ring lizard and snake-skin" are solely "for the *foot* if" (in the voice's tart bite) "you see *fit*" because now "you" are being tutored not in unastonished openness but in the rhyme-hard closure that toughly insists "they've *cats* not cobras / to keep down the *rats*." The poem is now more clearly moving from broad permissiveness to the tightly circumspect—from the large embrace of Dürer's sea-view and varied palette to the sterner, monochrome outlook of Ambrose. In his more reproving foreignness, this college student, "with his not-native books and hat," and bearing the name, as Slatin observes,[21] of the Milanese saint who kept back heretical incursions on the early Church, "sees" from his hillside height "boats // at sea progress white and rigid as if / in a groove"—a non-deviating strictness of viewpoint that makes "the pitch of the church // spire, not true" appear to be an architectural and moral swerving from the upright.

Yet such rigidity leads Moore to adjust again: not swinging back to Dürer's broad spectrum of color but to the moral color-changes associated with a nimble, native steeplejack who comes down, unlike Ambrose, from a religious height. With him the poem is more dexterously adapting to what Moore once called "life's faulty excellence" in "To Statecraft Embalmed," now that the ability to ride across wildness and formality in their privileging confusion has become the means to maintain an ethical sureness of step, worth nothing unless it is perilously balanced. So in a descent which might be seen as a human fall,

> a man in scarlet lets
> down a rope as a spider spins a thread

—the rope unreeled with the alliterative ease of a *spider-spinning* tale that makes man a scarlet sinner, before the next line moderates the idea into fiction and lets him step unfictitiously down to earth:

> he might be part of a novel, but on the sidewalk a
> sign says C.J. Poole, Steeple-Jack,
>   in black and white; and one in red
> and white says
>
> Danger.

But even though an unextravagant "black and white" takes over from scarlet when "a / sign says" (a saying to *see* in sidewalk plainness) "C.J. Poole Steeple-Jack," the emphatic addition of "a *red* and white" sign—forcibly saying "*Danger*," with the word suddenly standing out on the page—alters the seen/spoken picture again. The temptations of human frailty are not to be forgotten, though colored in "red and white" rather than scarlet excess, just as the thought of whited sepulchres in the church portico "made modester / by whitewash" may come to mind, only to be banished by such modesty. Here, after all, is a "fit haven" (but not in sardonic foot-fittingness) "for / waifs, children, animals, prisoners . . ." Prisoners, indeed? But the guilty suggestion vanishes as the voice trips quickly from "*prisoners*" to "*pres*idents who have repaid" (like Moore's political hero, President Hoover)[22] "*sin*-driven // *sen*ators" (in the acoustic downslide of the congressionally remissive) "by not thinking about them."

Such unpunitive abandon goes with the last stanza's pleasure in civic virtues whose value has been enhanced by Moore's accentuation of spiritual risk. The disaster-accepting, vocal blitheness that earlier made the stranded whales a "reason" for living here is now succeeded by the greater certainty of the declaration:

> It could not be dangerous to be living
>   in a town like this . . .

Insisting that it "*could* not be dangerous" (unlike the weakening of sureness in her 1941 recorded version, where "It *scarcely* could be" so),[23] Moore's tone and sound-play ride on the sense of perils' real potentiality in this town

>   of simple people,
>   who have a steeple-jack placing danger-signs by the church

in all its possible yet guarded-against pride. For the "*people*," it is insisted, have their "*steeple*-jack" protector who, in his athletic straddling of suggestion, is down below, while above

>   he is gilding the solid-
>   pointed star, which on a steeple
>   stands for hope.

Not gilding the lily in sublime excess, he is "gil*ding*," in hard-edged concreteness, "the solid- / pointed star"—the "*star*" which cannot complacently soar too high, in terms of moral loftiness, but points to the word-tight limits of what it does mean, here and now, when, "on a *stee*ple," it "*sta*nds for hope." Like Mount Rainier's goat, the small line "stands its ground": no stand-in for the transcendent, but the firm footing by which sound and spirit, vivified by danger and animal alacrity, find grounds for living in a place like this.

Six

Quick, Said the Bird

"[T]he feeling for syllable and rhythm, penetrating far below the conscious levels of thought and feeling, invigorating every word; sinking to the most primitive and forgotten, returning to the origin and bringing something back."
ELIOT on the auditory imagination, 1933[1]

Because I think not ever to return,
Ballad, to Tuscany . . .
CAVALCANTI, "Ballata: In Exile at Sarzana"

Unlike Moore, the post-*Waste Land* Eliot had fewer grounds for living in his own country. He may have placed "The Steeple-Jack" first in his 1935 edition of her *Selected Poems* so that new readers would have a welcoming port of entry, but he could not join Williams in saying of the poem, "it is my own scene."[2] For he now seems at a distance from America, not by geography (a separation overcome in *The Waste Land*, after all, by the native resourcefulness of an exile, winning back the rhythms of possibility out of deadlock) but by putting himself at a greater spiritual remove. The Anglican convert of the 1930 *Ash-Wednesday* seems far away from previous quickenings via animal or bird: "Why should the agèd eagle stretch his wings?" Indeed his skepticism about outstretch appears so strong that he has little inclination to go against the process which, from "Burnt Norton" in 1935 to the 1942 "Little Gidding," undercuts the solid, sounded world and its temporal fruits—"Ridiculous the waste sad time / Stretching before and after."

But Eliot also surprises. In the earlier *Sweeney Agonistes* (begun 1923) he searches below words for the impulse of resurgence which, in *Waste Land* style, "shall bring / Sweeney to Mrs. Porter in the spring." After Sweeney's other evolutions, whether among the nightingales or as the matted ape of "Sweeney Erect" (1919) who turns into a clean-shaven species, the modern *Sacre du Printemps* might be succeeded in "Fragment of an Agon" by Eliot's version of an Aristophanic ἀγών—the "agon" struggle where life, as embodied by Sweeney, battles death by devouring it. As in the songs "Under the bamboo tree" and "My little island girl," sung by Eliot's assorted cast as they entice Doris to the auditory bareness of a tropical isle ("Nothing to hear" there, says Sweeney, "but the sound of surf"), language is only the debased necessity ("I gotta use words when I talk to you") by which to reach a raw, compulsive beat and a contest:

DORIS: That's not life, that's no life
               Why I'd just as soon be dead.
SWEENEY: That's what life is. Just is.
DORIS: What is?
       What's that life is?
SWEENEY: Life is death. (CPP, 123)

Close to the mechanistic jerkiness of the words-as-noise compulsion in the "nerves" section of *The Waste Land* ("What are you thinking of? What thinking? What?") such jog-trot rapidity ("Thát's nŏt . . . Thát's whăt"; " Júst iš . . . Whát iš") drives the "is" of Doris's crumbling grammar ("What's that life is?") into the snap-shut jaws of Sweeney's "Life is death"—so fast, in fact, that Eliot deliberately did not differentiate between the separate characters when he read the "Agon" to an audience, so as "to convey the sort of rhythm I intended."[3]

But the kind of rhythm he intended remains questionable. The dinning beat of Sweeney's manic insistences ("Any man might do a girl in . . . has to, needs to, wants to . . . do a girl in") is only leading to a deadly sense of fate in a caricature of American English: "We all gotta do what we gotta do." It is as if Eliot's attempt to escape inhibitions in order to find a deep, pulsating force that will urge him forward—like a creative destiny that exists "far below the conscious levels of thought and feeling, invigorating every word"—actually delivers him into shallows and a cruder acoustic. But these have a significance notably different from the one assigned by Michael North when he sees Eliot, like Williams in the alleged racial disguise of "Shoot it Jimmy!," assuming "a black voice to remake the English language."[4] For as characters in the "Agon" sing "Under the Bamboo Tree"—"Swarts as Tambo, Snow as Bones," like players on the tambourine and bones in a minstrel show—the truth is not that the distorting, exploitative Eliot, as North characterizes him, "imprisons the song once again in the minstrel tradition"[5] but that he is once more yielding to an oppression of the self, not of others, hammered down by the beat of a mechanistic unconscious. Always potentially there in the poetry from the early days, as with the "dull tom-tom" in "Portrait of a Lady" or the beat of each street lamp "like a fatalistic drum" in "Rhapsody on a Windy Night," it can only be a simulacrum of the mind's deeper, liberating rhythms, just as the children's song in "The Hollow Men" (1925), "*Here we go round the prickly pear / Prickly pear prickly pear*" can never be other than a futile, imprisoning jog compared to the sprightly nursery rhyme "London Bridge is falling down" in *The Waste Land*. Without such release, and caught in repetitive rigidities, *Sweeney Agonistes* therefore yields itself to the "primitive" note of Vachel Lindsay's cartoon Africa in "The Congo" ("BOOM, kill the white men, / Hoo, Hoo, Hoo") as Eliot descends from explicable language to the grunts of a terrible mockery ("Hoo ha ha / Hoo ha ha"). Paused on, sound by sound—

Hoo

Hoo

Hoo

—they belong to the level of dehumanized noise that Lindsay enjoys speedily ("CRACK, CRACK, CRACK") with the cars of the "The Santa-Fe Trail" but which Eliot replays as the slowly heard beats of menace at the door: "KNOCK / KNOCK / KNOCK." Indeed, what stands out is not the poet's black-voiced disguise but the sounds of doom that equally reverberate for him in Poe's tales. Despite his lack of explicit comment on those moments of terror instanced by Roderick Usher listening to the clashes that come from Madeline's tomb or by the murderer hearing an imagined throb ("hark! louder! *louder!*") from inside his victim in "The Tell-Tale Heart," the same underground kind of acoustics are at work in the verse of Poe that he does applaud. These have, he says, "the effect of an incantation which, because of its very crudity, stirs the feelings at a deep and almost primitive level":[6] a "power of incantation" in Poe's "Ulalume"[7] which we may indeed verify in the insistent cry of "Ulalume, Ulalume" (or "Oo-la-loom," as every syllable is dragged out for its melodrama) "Tis the vault of thy lost Ulalume!" Poe's "For Annie" also casts its auditory spell on Eliot by the "naive beat" that "goes on throbbing in your head"[8] (to be verified again by the calculated repetitions of "The moaning and groaning, / The sighing and sobbing . . . that horrible, / Horrible throbbing"). Distinct from Eliot's enjoyment of unsophisticated rhythms in the poetry of Kipling and John Davidson, nursery rhymes, or songs from American vaudeville and English music hall,[9] the espousing of the "primitive level" via Poe can only be a surrender to somnambulistic dictates.

But for Eliot, the assimilator and surpassor of automatisms in *The Waste Land*, there are yearnings which spring from deeper sources and move him in a different emotional direction. For just as the Kaluli of New Guinea find their way back to memories and places they have left by retracing the "poetic song paths" described by Steven Feld[10]—routes taking them home to a real and felt geography, significantly overseen by the spirit presence of a bird[11]— and just as Australia's indigenous people remember "songlines" when they find their way without maps across vast distances, so the acoustics calling Eliot back from exile represent a less ritualized counterpart. The poet at the start of *Ash-Wednesday* who, in an echo of Cavalcanti's "Perch'io non spero," hopes not to turn is the same person who, in an act of *return*, originally gave *Ash-Wednesday* the title of "All Aboard for Natchez Cairo and St. Louis": the cry of a train conductor to passengers, together with the ringing of a bell and the hooting of a locomotive, in the comic dialogue performed by the black entertainers Moran and Mack.[12] Delighting in their 1928 recording, word by word,[13] the Eliot who can lament in *Ash-Wednesday* that "time is always time

/ And place is always and only place" (Tiresias-like disparagings of existence that earn Williams's specific denunciation as "The Fatal Blunder")[14] can also reach out, in full vigor, to a scene that his prose cherishes and remembers from his New England boyhood: "the bay and goldenrod, the song-sparrows, the red granite and the blue sea."[15] Once more the place is there in the poem when the mouth's articulating zest opens a "*wide window*" and—with word prompting word to further expanse, like "Red sails / *Wide* to lee*ward*" in *The Waste Land*—ventures on the "sea*ward*" flight of "*wide* sails":

> From the wide window towards the granite shore
> The wide sails still fly seaward, seaward flying (CPP, 89)

—"*flying*" pushed into greater emphasis by the second "seaward," and followed by "Unbroken wings." It as if those "*wings*" must not break the *wide*-flying momentum of delight which has escaped Eliot's world-renouncing Christianity. He must try not to lose his verbal hold on a sense of release, even though now, by contrast with the spontaneous upwelling that led him to the hermit-thrush of "What the Thunder Said," he has to be stubbornly persistent:

> And the lost heart stiffens and rejoices
> In the lost lilac and the lost sea voices
> And the weak spirit quickens to rebel

—a clutched-at trail of sound and reviving strength, asserted, bit by bit, with "And . . . and." So "sea v*oices*" fasten upon "rej*oices*" with the extra rhymed pressure that sends "reb*el*" grasping more urgently at the unlost "sea-sm*ell*" in the next stanza, as the senses are sharpened. And what "quickens to rebel // For the bent golden-rod and the lost sea-smell" more acutely

> Quickens to recover

—to "*recover*": the special emphasis in this word-track that has the force to summon up

> The cry of quail and the whirling plover

It is a "whirling" that Eliot rescues from his previous denigration in *Ash-Wednesday* where "the unstilled world still whirled / About the centre of the silent Word." For the words used by the speaking voice to utter this world—to reclaim it, piece by piece—persist in rivaling for the moment any attachment to an unspoken, transcendent Logos. In "Marina," the same year as *Ash-Wednesday*, the bereft Pericles follows the other bereaved Shakespearean prince of City and river in *The Waste Land* by reclaiming a sea and coast, though one with an American identity, Rogue Island in Maine's Casco Bay,[16] which has special youthful memories for Eliot. Therefore, while Seneca's Hercules Furens in the poem's Latin epigraph wakes in a daze from his god-induced madness and is on the verge of realizing that he has killed his children ("What is this place, what land, what region of the world?"), Pericles wakes to the greater specifics of a landfall and a recoverable child—everything, in fact, that the poet, by sight, smell, and sound, has not quite killed in himself through adherence to his own God:

> What seas what shores what grey rocks and what islands
> What water lapping the bow
> And scent of pine and the woodthrush singing through the fog
> What images return
> O my daughter (CPP, 109)

Not fact, then, but "images"? However, each "What," or each urging-forth by the creative unconscious, is bringing the world's parts back into individually realized substance. So too the mouth-widening breath of "*What water*" moves with the "*woo*dthrush singing through the fog" as it cuts through the haze with more agile animality than the fixed images of lustful horror which break in upon Pericles for a moment: the mechanistic symmetries of thought which make him contemplate "Those who sharpen the teeth of the dog, meaning / Death" or "Those who suffer the ecstasy of the animals." As such images "become unsubstantial, reduced by a wind, / A breath of pine, and the woodsong fog," the wood in that song implies a different birdlike substance and a child looming through the mind's mist ("What is this face, less clear and clearer . . . ?"), all before she fleets away with "Whispers and small laughter between leaves and hurrying feet," like the chuckle of the ghost-child in Kipling's "They."[17] But the scurry of assonance ("*lea*ves . . . *fee*t") keeps speech on track through the unconscious—"Under *slee*p, where all the waters *mee*t" to the "*hea*t" and "ice" of the external mind's voyaging and beyond:

> Bowsprit cracked with ice and paint cracked with heat.
> I made this, I have forgotten
> And remember.
> [. . .]
> Between one June and another September.

Below the aged surface of mental symmetry, another pulse beats. The line that rises on "cracked with ice" and falls on "cracked with heat" has a smaller arc inside it, lifting on "forgotten," descending on "remember," and letting a fresher remembrance of time emerge in the rise-fall span that goes from "one June" to "another September." "I made this," says Pericles (and his poet, a "devoted bird-watcher" as a boy in coastal New England "from June to October"):[18] the statement itself forgotten, only to be remembered as "Made this unknowing," where *"unknowing"* stresses the impulse that would reach out from old, dead knowledge to the child who can be claimed, "half conscious, unknown," as "my *own*" in emphatic closeness.

But by now the inner, refreshing rhythms have vanished, and language in the poem becomes a series of thinning insistences. Marina has changed, abstractly, into "This form, this face, this life" for which Pericles would resign his old life, and though he would forsake his "speech for that unspoken," with "lips parted" to utter "the hope, the new ships," the breath expires on a gesture toward newness rather than gaining the felt, substantial thing. Even as the shore's hard rock presses closer to the ship's wooden keel ("what granite islands towards my timbers") the woodthrush "calling through the fog" belongs now to a distant, plaintive yearning for an impromptu life or a childike zest that Eliot finds increasingly difficult to voice in the poetry. Thus the child and authority figure of "Coriolan" (1931) may want "the sweep of the little bat's wing" but an up-down rhythm cannot be coaxed into action. "'Rising and falling, crowned with dust,' the small creatures, / The small creatures"—as he repetitively tries to will them to a greater sound—"chirp thinly through the dust" (CPP, 130).

It is a deadlocked state where Moore's example notably becomes important in rousing Eliot from stasis. The abrupt leaps of the "sand-brown jumping-rat" in her 1932 poem "The Jerboa," to which he gives early prominence in the *Selected Poems* by placing it third, can be suggested by "the uneven notes / of the Bedouin flute"—a people's nimble art animalistically pitted against the reductive aesthetics of Rome or Pharaoh—just as an animal-enlivening artifact, a Dresden china swan,[19] can be played against a haughty live bird and royal stultification in "No Swan So Fine" from the same year:

"No water so still as the
    dead fountains of Versailles." No swan,
with swart blind look askance
and gondoliering legs, so fine
    as the chintz china one with fawn-
brown eyes . . . (PMM, 189)

Waiting out the time from "so still" to "so fine," Moore has the assured dexterity which can swing back upon the "swart bl*i*nd look" with what is distinctively "*fine*" in the "ch*i*na" bird, and cuttingly so. For the gleaming shift of faceted vowels from /i/ to /ai/ ("ch*i*ntz ch*i*na") shines with the lifelike acuity of look enacted by the sound-change from "*fine*" to "*fawn-* / brown eyes."

Placing this poem almost immediately after "The Jerboa" in the *Selected*, Eliot seems to have noted it with special interest. Back in America (1932–1933) after a gap of seventeen years, he has before him a suggestion of the way that he too, with patience, might probe a seemingly torpid surface. The "dead fountains" of Moore's poem (first published in October 1932) can therefore become the river in "Virginia" (written April/May 1933):

> Red river, red river
> Slow flow heat is silence
> No will is still as a river
> Still. Will heat move
> Only through the mocking-bird
> Heard once? (CPP, 139)

But movement is impeded. "Red river, red river" is held fast by repetition, and the will cannot be unclogged either by the stilling internal rhymes or the "will-Will" homophone. Any stirring has to be through the sound of the avian imitator who replaces Moore's imitation swan—the mockingbird differentiated from the flat sameness of "Slow flow . . . No" (and "-bird / heard") by being heard "Only . . . once" with the one-and-only possibility of escape that Eliot knew in *The Waste Land*: "I have heard the key / Turn in the door once and turn once only." But in "Virginia" the door stays shut on inmost feelings. Everything that stirs also remains the same, like "Ever moving / Iron thoughts" that "came with me / And go with me."

Yet there, in the small to-and-fro—

> came with me
> go with me

—one hears the faint urging of a beat that Eliot could nurture further in "New Hampshire" written shortly after in June 1933. Moore heard an "indigenous rhythm" in the poem,[20] and we may note how the home-rooted sound of "Children's voices in the orchard" under the protective canopy of birds ("Black wing, brown wing, hover over") lets Eliot create a small momentum from a simple to-and-fro:

> Golden head, black wing,
> Cling, swing,
> Spring, sing,
> Swing up into the apple tree. (CPP, 138)

So, indeed, the voice mounts by rhyme and differentiation to "Swing *up* into the *app*le tree." Behind "New Hampshire," moreover, lie other indigenous rhythms, as when Whitman builds an upsurge by adverbially renewing each line-start and evokes his listening as a child to the lonely bird who sings for its mate:

> Out of the cradle endlessly rocking,
> Out of the mocking-bird's throat, the musical shuttle,

> Out of the Nine-month midnight,
> Over the sterile sands and the fields beyond . . . (*Leaves of Grass*, 196)

Lines such as these, together with Whitman's montage amassing of "processions," "countless torches," and "sombre faces" in the Lincoln elegy, once notably affected Eliot in *The Waste Land*. Rearing up each adverbial line at the start of "What the Thunder Said" ("After the torchlight red on sweaty faces / After the frosty silence . . . After the agony . . .") the voice winds its way (as does Whitman, with his simple "sprig of lilac" for Lincoln) to the modesty of "a little patience" and thence to a more ardent climb.

But a year after "New Hampshire" Eliot has turned against the search for the genuinely deeper pulse by which he might rise again. Accordingly, in his Anglican church pageant *The Rock,* he cuts back in parody of Whitman's large-breathed "O-u-t of . . . O-u-t of" so that a stricter "order" may issue from it:

> Out of the slimy mud of words, out of the sleet and hail of verbal imprecisions,
> Approximate thoughts and feelings, words that have taken the place of thoughts
>   and feelings,
> There spring the perfect order of speech, and the beauty of incantation.
>   (CPP, 164)

This is no "Spring, sing" but a return to the rigors that Eliot had applauded in his 1926 "Note Sur Mallarmé et Poe." For him, the "incantation" of these poets "insists on the primitive power of the Word (*Fatum*)":[21] the "primitive" in Poe's verse especially appealing to that auditory side of Eliot which, failing to be guided by a deeper, subtler rhythm, likes to be driven by what seems unalterable fate or mechanistic compulsion.[22] It is no surprise, therefore, that the incantatory style of Poe resonates behind the last of the *Quartets*, "Little Gidding," as the poetry strides toward the timelessly phantasmal after a London air raid. Where the melodrama of "Ulalume" beats a way "down by the dank tarn of Auber, / In the ghoul-haunted woodland of Weir," the sound of fated inevitability, helped by Dantean *terza rima*, can now overlay Whitman's upheaving line-starts and syntactic suspense ("Out of the cradle . . . Out of the mocking-bird's throat . . . Over the sterile sands . . .") with the adverbial units ("In the uncertain hour before . . . At the recurrent end of . . . Over the asphalt where . . .") that balefully subvert time's sureness:

> In the uncertain hour before the morning
>   Near the ending of interminable night
>   At the recurrent end of the unending
> After the dark dove with the flickering tongue
>   Had passed below the horizon of his homing

While the dead leaves still rattled on like tin
Over the asphalt where no other sound was (CPP, 191)

Up goes the voice ("uncertain *hour*," "ending," and "recurrent *end*"). Down it comes again just as inevitably on *"morning,"* "interminable *night,"* and "the *unending*": all part of the verse-line arc which, in the rise of "dark dove" and the fall-back on "flickering tongue," also shows how Eliot has made his bird-quickened sense of language into a fork-tongued duality. Divine love yet earthly pain; Holy Ghost yet enemy raider: the "dark dove" (the peace of whose "hom*ing*" is hit against by the clatter of the blown leaves' "*tin*") has its dualistic successor when the sentence finds its verb at last and the "compound ghost" is met by the "I" of a "double part."

This, though, is not the "I" who emerges out of the City crowd to greet Stetson with a mixture of scorn and friendship. That conflict of feelings, in attempted human outreach to another, makes the duality of the later "meeting nowhere, no before and after" seem emotionally unrooted in comparison (with the exception of the tirade launched by Eliot's "exasperated spirit" against life's empty rewards and the "bitter tastelessness of shadow fruit"). The "I's" plausible cry to the ghost, "'What! are *you* here' / Although we were not," is totally different from the City street recognition of "Stetson! / You who were with me in the ships at Mylae!" because this is no jocund spanning of historic distances by the here-and-now voice, but a means of clothing the unearthly and timeless in the guise of solid substance. One can see now why Eliot in his article on Poe and Mallarmé relished the "firmness" of the verbal "steps by which they pass" so convincingly "from the tangible world to the world of phantoms."[23] Indeed the concrete-seeming sound has no value except as a plausible way to avoid the suggestion of ghostly flimsiness. So, without floating,[24] "We trod the pavement in a dead patrol," where the force of "*trod*" (like the vivifying effect of "*sudden*" on "*some dead*" in "the sudden look of some dead master") provides life's stamp to authenticate the strange "pa*trol*."

All this is anticipated seven years before in "Burnt Norton" when Eliot uses the speaking voice to make unembodied things—the *not* done—seem to tread so solidly:

Footfalls echo in the memory
Down the passage which we did not take
Towards the door we never opened
Into the rose-garden. My words echo
Thus, in your mind. (CPP, 171)

The sound of such words is the contradictory way to eternal silence and stillness. But it is also the way to convince the ear and mind that the trochaic "Footfalls" are not bodiless echoes (as they are) but the weight that directs us unswervingly, with another initial stress, "*Down* the passage which we did not take": a route nevertheless taken, as if it were real, through "the door we never opened," yet which we are indeed imaginatively opening at this very moment, ushered by a further trochee "*In*to the rose-garden." Even when Eliot makes plain, by more line-start stress, that it is only his words, not facts, which "echo / *Thus*, in your mind," his change from "we" to an I-and-you intimacy softens the reminder that he deals in echoes rather than substance. It cannot seem too negative when the sense of shriveled futility he intimates—"But to what purpose / Disturbing the dust on a bowl of rose-leaves"—is immediately left behind by the modesty of "I do not know." Nor can the mind stay to pause on the thought that "Other echoes," not substantial things, "Inhabit the garden." For now the voice asks "Shall we follow?," inviting us to speed in hide-and-seek delight "Round the corner" of each verse-line:

> Quick, said the bird, find them, find them,
> Round the corner. Through the first gate,
> Into our first world, shall we follow
> The deception of the thrush? Into our first world,
> There they were . . .

"They" are "dignified, invisible" elders who "were" here: a past tense seeming so present, but which, when led to by the future-denoting "shall" (as "Words . . . slip, slide . . . Decay with imprecision, will not stay in place") becomes a timeless moment mystically glimpsed before "they" vanish. But to reach that point, we must obey a bird whose "Quick" insistences are only echoes ("find them, find them") of a spontaneous quickening. Eliot may once have imitated the hermit-thrush ("Drip drop drip drop") but there he ardently yearned for refreshment in this life, while here his repetitions echoing the bird in "first . . . first" (then nonstop "Into our first world" and again "Into our first world") speedily beguile us into temporal satisfaction that is deemed a falsity. For the childlike, bird-inspired delight is about to be betrayed when, with the mystic moment ended, we can no longer ignore the "deception of the thrush":

> Go said the bird, for the leaves were full of children
> Hidden excitedly, containing laughter.
> Go, go, go, said the bird: human kind
> Cannot bear very much reality.

Now banishment cancels eager invitation: a cruel casting-out at the very moment of brimming possibility. "Go," says this harbinger of the "dark dove with the flickering tongue," "*for* the leaves were full of children"—indeed, we must go *because* there is such plenty and *because* the nonstop spoken sentence has joyed so much in the yet-to-be-unfolded, "Hidden excitedly, containing laughter." That, above all, has to be cut against by the dualistic voice, harsh-

QUICK, SAID THE BIRD 99

ened as it more fervently insists, "Go, go, go" and announces, with Tiresian hauteur, that "human kind" is unable to bear "very much" of that supposed "reality." If "reality" is time's plenitude turned empty in a flash, then "the hidden laughter / Of children in the foliage" at the end of "Burnt Norton" is another warning of laughter about to be shut down rather than the containment of potentially spilling delight. We do not need a bird to urge us forward again when Eliot says, with apparent time-valuing urgency, "Quick, now, here, now, always" (with "alw-a-ys" lingering so positively after the rapid monosyllables), then cuts straight away to "Ridiculous the waste sad time / Stretching" (as the stretched-out, tired obverse of "always") "before and after."

Yet "quick quick quick," says Eliot, surprising us again. For world-weariness is essentially not the sound which emanates from the poem "Cape Ann" which he wrote *after* "Burnt Norton" in late 1935.[25] The deceptive thrush is here replaced by birds of the American northeast coast, and their calls are pursued not in self-conscious echoings ("Shall we follow? . . . shall we follow . . . ?") but by the eager directness that, taking its cue from the car sounds italicized by Lindsay in "The Santa-Fé Trail" ("Hark to the *calm*-horn, *balm*-horn, *psalm*-horn. / Hark to the *faint*-horn, *quaint*-horn, *saint*-horn"), urges:

> O quick quick quick, quick hear the song-sparrow
> Swamp-sparrow, fox-sparrow, vesper-sparrow
> At dawn and dusk. Follow the dance
> Of the goldfinch at noon. Leave to chance
> The Blackburnian warbler, the shy one . . . (CPP, 142)

Following such song paths, Eliot is here brought back to the midst of native ground with a keenness rivaling Whitman's when he listens in *Specimen Days* to the individual notes of catbird, meadowlark, quail, hawk, and kingfisher by the Delaware River. But the poet of "Cape Ann" needs the upswoop of the initial "quick's" to carry forward the singling-out of each sparrow's distinctness before the voice falls away on "dawn" and "dusk." In the same way, before the voice lapses again on "noon" and "the shy one," he must renew the fast, up-curving impulse ("Follow the dance," "Leave to chance") because the fall-to-rise beat, not its up-down mechanistic imitation, is once more invigoratingly emergent, as "Hail" starts the quick climb of the voice-arc in order to rhyme with another bird:

> Hail
> With shrill whistle the note of the quail, the bob-white
> Dodging by bay-bush . . .

According to Frank Chapman, whose comment on the hermit thrush's "purity of tone" is quoted by Eliot in the notes to *The Waste Land*, the quail gained its other name from the spring call of the male as "he whistles the two clear musical, ringing notes *Bob-white!*"[26] For Eliot this demands the lip-pursed force of *"whistle"* for "bob-*white"* where the bounce of plosives tracks the *"Dodging"* of the *"bob*-white . . . by bay-bush."* Close-hugging fricatives also adhere to the different movements of waterthrush and purple martin: "Follow the *feet* . . . Follow the *flight* . . ." While that matches a bird's walk or dance, it is equally proper to "Greet / In silence" the unheard nighthawk or bullbat. But there terseness brakes the onrush. "All are delectable," and "quick quick quick" is replaced by the fond slowing-down of "Sweet sweet sweet." Indeed, the time has come for such Hopkinsian wordplay to be abandoned, with a borrowing from the other poet's farewell in "The Leaden Echo and the Golden Echo": "Come then, your ways and airs and looks . . . sweet looks, loose locks . . . Resign them, sign them" (verse read by Eliot himself to a Bryn Mawr audience in 1933):[27]

> But resign this land at the end, resign it
> To its true owner, the tough one, the sea-gull. (CPP, 130)

Vocal adaptation to a bird's individuality continues to the last, however. Without fleetness or a whistle-like note, "resign . . . resign it" has the firm brusqueness suiting the "true owner"—curtly "the tough one" and in trenchant finality "the sea-gull." Snapping shut the poem ("The palaver is finished")[28] Eliot equally resigns from voicing a native ground or landfall. With the seagull he looks to "the empty desolation, / The wave cry, the wind cry, the vast waters / Of the petrel and the porpoise" in "East Coker": an Atlantic voyaged by his English ancestor going to the New World, where the tolling funeral bell of the "groaner" buoy in "The Dry Salvages" belongs with the descant of a voice "not to the ear . . . and not in any language." In such endless journeys without arrival, and the ascent of words into silence, the only genuine utterable ground is now as distant as the "voice of the hidden waterfall" in "Little Gidding" and the sound of the "half-heard" children in the apple tree.

Nevertheless, there is a home ground to be reached and voiced. What Eliot abandons in "Cape Ann," Moore takes up the same year in "Virginia Britannia" (1935) when she continues the "palaver" with a land. Unlike Eliot's view of Virginia in *After Strange Gods* where he imagines that "the chances for the re-establishment of a native culture" are better than in New York or New England because it has been "less industrialised and less invaded by foreign races,"[29] the Old Dominion for her is a place of coexistences. In a notable passage from the poem, to be read aloud with one sustained breath, foreign colonizers and native inhabitants historically live side by side on "the cedar-dotted emerald shore / known to the redbird, / the redcoated musketeer" (their colors indistinguishable) and "the trumpet-flower, the cavalier": all in joint flamboyance. It is the same juxtaposing delight which follows through the link between the civilized and the wild in Jefferson's curving design at the University of Virginia, whose "one-brick-thick- // wall serpentine shadows star- / tle strangers": a "brick-thick" insistence as undeviating, in verbal tightness, as "shadows startle strangers," where the latter noun almost touches "Strangler" or "The strangler fig" in the same line. Botanical kin to past exploiters and slavers "taking what they / pleased—colonizing as we say," the plant belongs to that sense of stark adjacencies, of opposites tensed against each other, so evident to Moore in American history, where violent human predators stanzaically occupy the same ground as the cultivation represented by "The limestone tea-table, / The mandoline-shaped big / and little fig."

But it is a bird who most gives body to Moore's vocal sense of wild and fold huddled against each other, as untamed energies reside next to, and become almost indistinguishable from, civilized control:

> Observe the terse Virginian,
>   the mettlesome gray one that drives the
>   owl from tree to tree and imitates the call
> of whippoorwill or
>   lark or katydid—the lead-
>   gray lead-legged mocking-bird with head
> held half away, and
>   meditative eye as dead
>   as sculptured marble
> eyes. Alighting noiseless-
> ly it muses
> in the semi-sun, on tall thin legs,
> as if it did not see,
>   still standing there alone
>   on the round stone-
> topped table with lead cupids grouped to
>   form the pedestal. (*Life and Letters Today*, December 1935)

Observing "the terse Virginian" in the taut command of a sentence, we must also follow through the "mettlesome" attack on the owl and the imitation of other birds, before speech is slowed to mimic the mockingbird's own faux-petrifaction. For at "katy*did*" each *d*-hard segment of the hyphenated adjective and noun demands such paused-upon emphasis—as in "the lead- / gray lea*d*-legge*d* mockingbird" where "-*legged*" stresses its doubly *lead*en guise—that the "*head*" seems to stiffen in movement: the "*head* / *held half* away" now allowing only the smallest of inclination, and the "meditative eye as d*ead*," in its lead-head firmness of rhyme and feigned statuesque fixity, as "sculptured marble / eyes." Yet the mimic's "*eye*" of life remains un-marmoreal through the "marble / *eyes*," and is intimated further by "A*lighting*" as the deft creature, "Alighting noiseless- / *ly*" with the line-break's tiptoe care, adapts to, indeed completes, the man-made objects of garden civility. Musing "as if it did not see" (in quiet chime with "noiseless- / ly") and "*still* s*t*anding . . . on the . . . s*t*one-" ("alone" in rhyming sameness with the "s*t*one- / *t*opped table) it nevertheless lightens heaviness with its "tall thin legs." More springy than any "lead-head-dead" remembrance, those "lead cu*p*ids," after "*t*o*pp*ed," are "cu*p*ids gr*o*u*p*ed to form," in the final bird-stone effect, "the PEDestal."

But the wild bird's choosing restraint is markedly different from the self-taming ascribed to animals in Moore's later verse, where her attenuations are comparable to Eliot's. His animal quickenings harden into a vision of the deceptive thrush and a symbolic "dark dove" through disbelief in the virtues of the bodied world—a land only valuable through its intersection with the timeless—while Moore's creatures of self-surrender emerge from the collapse of vital opposites in her nature. The interplay between force and delicacy, outer zest and inner privacy, has vanished when, in the cause of spiritual relinquishing, she turns the ferocious into the emollient, but only, as Robert Duncan suggests, by pretending to speak from strength.[30] Staunchness can only ring out through the wordplay chimes of the pleasantly amenable when Maine's non-fighting porcupine ("Apparition of Splendor," 1952) is lauded in the face of an enemy: "Shallow oppressor, intruder / insister, you have found a resister" (PMM, 282). So, too, when the selfless surrender of the happy prisoner is better than unbowed resilience, and the supposed "mighty singing" of the captive bird in "What Are Years?" (1940, PMM 237) comes down to the lamer pleasure of saying, "satisfaction is a lowly / thing, how pure a thing is joy" (with all the verbal blankness of the repeated "thing" that "joy" cannot color). Indeed, robust expectations are to be deliberately deflated, like a more audience-friendly version of the misleadings in "An Octopus" and other poems, when, as an introduction to the "life prisoner but reconciled" who obediently carries the Buddha's tooth in the 1944 "Elephants"—now that the more assertive beast of "Black Earth" is soon to be disavowed[31]—she heaps up the entanglement of two elephants' trunks ("the opposing opposed") and teases the reader with the thought that such oppositions mean war. Is this "a / knock-down drag-out fight that asks no quarter?" Not so, in fact. "Just / a pastime" (PMM, 255).

But such tossed-away amusement is not at all the same as her earlier quick cutting from one aspect of a lizard to another in "The Plumet Basilisk" (1932). For this is the "dragon" defender of unmaterialistic gold who

> as you look begins to be a
> nervous naked sword on little feet, with three-fold
> separate flame above the hilt, inhabiting

—yet fearlessly "in*h*abiting," across the stanza-space, the sharp unaspirate bite of—

fire *eating* into *air*. (PMM, 196)

There speaks a remarkably different Moore: far from the kind of defeat which eulogizes the runaway ostrich of "He 'Digesteth Harde Yron'" (1941) and much nearer the resoluteness of the birds who catch Williams's eye in "The Maneuver" (1946):

> I saw the two starlings
> coming in toward the wires.
> But at the last,
> just before alighting, they
>
> turned in the air together
> and landed backwards!
> that's what got me—to
> face into the wind's teeth (CWP2, 141)

It is a defiant partnering of the world that Williams especially grasps by short-line constraint: the tightness that illuminates the acoustic clustering of "*two . . . to*ward," "*together*" and "*to* / face." Abbreviation also prolongs the birds' airy hovering before they reach the wires, when Williams's earlier draft version ("at the last moment")[32] has its noun omitted, so that "la*st*" becomes an upstress which then lifts "ju*st* before alighting" into a balanced suspense: the *a*, *l*, and *t* of "at the last" lingeringly echoed in "alighting," while "they," the birds, textually hang in space at the line-break. But, as "they // turned in the air together," the squeezing of sounds is such (the *ur* of "turned" brought close to "*air*" and the *er* of "together") that Williams's high-pitched cry of amazement in "landed backwards!" comes as a release. It goes with the exclamatory rightness with which he rises, step by step in his 1954 reading[33] to say, "that's what got *me*"—not the anticlimactic downchime of "wh*at got* me" but the high emphasis that matches the birds' synchronized landing and their tight-knit poise against the wind. So, at the last, in a two and two dance of words, the ferocity of the "wind's *tee*th" is, by the line-jutting "*to*," undauntedly faced "in*to*."

In all this, Williams shows clearly how much the speaking voice of his postwar poetry can still draw on the resources that are now largely beyond Moore and Eliot. But he who is to suffer his own poetic enervations is only able to stay in touch with his powers if he keeps faith with the instinctive need to be, in outward reach and pull-back, a dexterous dance partner with the factual world beyond the self. The capacity is still there when the unbroken drive of onward speech, tensed to centripetal poise by short-line form cutting against it, depicts the "stubborn man" who embodies the coastal rocks, those "jagged ribs / riding the cloth of foam" in "Seafarer" (1948, CWP2 114). Inviting the storm, he

lives by it! instinct
with fears that are not fears
but prickles of ecstasy,
a secret liquor, a fire
that inflames his blood to

—to "coldness," however, in the next line-turn surprise, with each small, insistent /i/ (lives, instinct, prickles, liquor, inflames) urging the syntax on to jumps of unpredictability inside a controlled verse-shape. For despite an inflammatory crackle ("prickles of ecstasy, / a secret liquor") and the push against boundaries—

> so that the rocks
> seem rather to leap
> at the sea than the sea
> to envelope them. They strain
> forward to grasp ships

—a quick twist of discrimination inside form's tight walls neither lets the seafarer-artist engulf what he leaps toward or to be engulfed. Instead, in the close match of reacher and reached, as "the sky itself . . . bends down to be torn" upon those rocks, Williams again grips the separate parts under pressure as he did, long before, with the tree branches of "Spring Strains" where "Vibrant bowing limbs / pull downward, sucking in the sky." By the same continuity, it is a partnering that he once more strains toward, amidst his own adversities, in the poetry of his last phase, from the 1950s to the 1960s. But difficulties obstruct. How far he can regain the verve of the spoken relation without sentimental slackening or diversion; how far his surviving powers indeed reveal what also endures in the most vital verse of Eliot and Moore: these are the questions now central to the concluding chapter.

seven

A Way to the Last Leaftip

Unbroken speech cut against by short-line discipline; the jagged denial of easy harmony to the visual-vocal compound thus created: the necessary tensions of Williams's earlier poetry should not be forgotten when we come to his final phase. Like the farmer in Poem III of *Spring and All*, planning his crop amidst his blank fields and facing a cold wind—"composing / —antagonist" (the latter word tautly rapped out against the former)—Williams needs the crisscross of opposites that forbid the relaxation of the verse-line into neat phrasal compartments. It is a standard to remember in face of the later work: the keeping of an unslackened initiative which makes his 1943 poem "A Sort of a Song" especially distinctive. For here, where line-endings are scissored at non-obvious points in the spoken sentence, language's keen edges are continually exposed, or dart out from cover:

> Let the snake wait under
> his weed
> and the writing
> be of words, slow and quick, sharp
> to strike, quiet to wait,
> sleepless.
> —through metaphor to reconcile
> the people and the stones.
> Compose. (No ideas
> but in things) Invent!
> Saxifrage is my flower that splits
> the rocks. (CWP2, 55)

These, then, are the several ways to "reconcile / the people"—the poet's audience and Williams himself—with the hard, factual "stones" of the non-human world: *Saxifraga* erupting with sudden actuality from under its etymological surface, while the other creature of the potent word emerges with assonantal unhurriedness. Thus "Let the snake wait under / his weed," but not with the over-pat visual arrangement of "wait / under his weed." A potentially tidy balance must also be avoided by lineal asymmetry in "slow and quick, sharp / to strike" so that the unpredictable word-snake or "writing" hits its aim, recoils, and by a tight acoustic trajectory gets ready for the next pounce—

"*quick*" prompting "str*i*ke," the latter crowdedly constrained by "*q*uiet" so that "quiet to wait" implies no quiescence but, in the abruptly said "sleepless," a verbal vigilance. Word-on-word crush in the second stanza also demands that "st*o*nes" are pressed hard by "Comp*o*se" as the tightly bracketed, pre-*Paterson* maxim, "N*o* ideas / but in things" blocks the way to "Invent!" and to over-roomy metaphor. Forced to go by this narrow syntactic route, or via this impeding "stone," the voice, so intently "*in* th*i*ngs," can then more expansively but undiffusely "*In*-VENT!": the breath venting forth out of constriction the full outstretch of the Saxifrage sentence as the flower "splits / the rocks."

Having just recorded the poem for Kenneth Burke in June 1951, Williams declared: "[I]t's the idea that the poet and all he stands for . . . will prevail in the end. He's going to wait. He's a snake. He's a saxifrage. He's determined."[1] But that kind of determination is very different from the strenuous quelling of uncertainty about his powers heard in the poem "The Desert Music," which he recorded for Burke on the same occasion, and which he had just published by spoken performance a few days earlier at Harvard.[2] "I *am* a poet! I / am. I am," he cries; "I am a poet, I reaffirmed." For now, after his recent stroke and illness, it would seem that he feels less like a snake or saxifrage than the amorphous, prone figure seen on the bridge between El Paso and Juárez during a visit to Robert McAlmon. Self-described in a draft as "a kind of imitation of / a sack of rags that hides in itself / a music, a / possible music,"[3] he insists throughout the finished poem on the "music" that only he, allegedly, can hear. "What," he asks, ". . . can raise to my ear / so sweet a tune, built of such slime?," the "slime" in this case being an old naked dancer in a Juárez bar whose virginal idealization by the poem is followed by the exalting of a shapeless, fetus-like bundle on the bridge: "The music guards it . . . a protecting music." But while "the music volleys through as in / a lonely moment I hear it," it stays an undemonstrated insistence, pleaded for by the same poet who harks to the "certainty of music" supposedly emanating from the dead (*Hear! Hear them! / the Undying*") in the mountain grove of "A Unison" (1946). Whether far-off ancestral sound or the Juárez kind, it would in fact seem to derive its poetic lineage from the tantalizations of *Four Quartets*—"The unheard music hidden in the shrubbery" ("Burnt Norton") or the beguilement at a distance in "East Coker" that invokes the past's Hardyesque dancers: "If you do not come too close . . . you can hear the music / Of the weak pipe and the little drum."

Yet when we remember the close-up, audible concordances that Williams's poetry can achieve—the matching, by acoustics and verse-line, to fallen or disregarded fact—it is clear that the most genuinely earned "music" of "The Desert Music" is to be heard, not in clamorous yearnings, but these lines:

Only the poem.
Only the counted poem, to an exact measure:

to imitate, not to copy nature, not
to copy nature

NOT, prostrate, to copy nature
                    but a dance! to dance
two and two with him—
                sequestered there asleep,
                        right end up! (CWP2, 273)

Visual uprightness is there from the start: "Only" aligned with "Only"; "to
imitate" with "to copy." But by vocally loading the original bareness of "Only
the poem" with increasing syntactic weight, Williams wins the sound of a
greater, untoppled verticality. It is not just a "to / to" maintenance of poise (as
"to imitate" upholds, in acoustic-lineal trimness, "to an exact measure"). For
those "to's" are pushing *to*ward statement's goal which—blocked by the anti-
representational negatives building to the staunchest cry, "NOT, prostrate, to
copy nature"—is attained with the positive's springy release, as the weight on
speech is dexterously balanced out by "a dance! to dance." At last the "*to's*"
find their truest, but more spacious, alignment, with a "*two* and *two*" relation:
Williams not pulled down by shapelessness nor calling after evanescent "music," but, as with the "sleepless" word in "A Sort of a Song," keeping a wakeful
partnership with sleeping nature, "right end up!" in voice and line.

At this point, significantly, he moves into the triadic layout which soon
has special importance for him. Having climbed from his own prostration
and stroke of 1951, and beginning to write poetry again the following year, he
would seem to regard the three-ply form he had briefly used in *Paterson II* as a
means of continuing at a more meditative pace, an earlier artistic parallelism
with the world. Looking back at the *Paterson* extract, he could also see it as a
line-by-line way of holding on to life—an acceptance of descent "made up of
despairs" as the way to "a reversal / of despair":

The descent beckons
            as the ascent beckoned
                    Memory is a kind
of accomplishment
            a sort of renewal
                    even
an initiation, since the spaces it opens are new places
            inhabited by hordes
                    heretofore unrealized,
of new kinds— (CWP2, 245)

But here comes a turning point in Williams's writing. The vocal-visual tensions of the past are yielding to an untautened visual organization on the

page. The "spaces it opens" are the white blanks in which the horizontal line of varying length (like the "varied foot" of Williams's later proclamations) is continually cut against, like a token version of his earlier line-slicings, by a vertical symmetry. With the flotations of the strung-out sentence thus meshed back into a grid of alignments, the spoken voice, no longer driving forward, is becoming the servant of a visually dominant script. For as Williams lays out the sentence in textually balanced units ("descent beckons": "ascent beckoned"; "inhabited": "unrealized") and makes the voice pause for an instant after "even"—the lone, hovering marker on the page—he offers a notational guide, in line-by-line scripting, to the way the poem should be read aloud. It is true that a vocal pressure still exists, independent of such neatening, as "*beckoned*" pushes forward to "*kind / of*" while the raised pitch of "*even*" lifts "*an initiation*," and "*hordes*" become, with aspirate force, "*heretofore* unrealized." But the sound of such definiteness operates amidst words that have become essentially indefinite, like the reusable "new" that variously prefaces "places," "kinds," "objectives," and "awakenings." Language like this is as disembodied in the poem as "Love without shadows . . . what is denied to love": all suggesting that Williams has lost in those abstract "shadows" a firmer sense of the "love" that can embrace difficulties and measure to the physical world with composition's vigor.

Aptly "The Descent," with that title, opens the 1954 collection *The Desert Music*, where three-ply form smoothes the way for shadowless love in "To Daphne and Virginia." After the concrete-sounding assertion which begins the poem ("The smell of the heat is boxwood") William edges forward *un*concretely with line-end pauses and scent-like stealth:

> a movement of the air
> stirs our thoughts
>   that had no life in them
>   to a life, a life in which
> two women agonize:
>   to live and to breathe is no less.
>   Two young women.
> The box odor
>   is the odor of that of which
>   partaking separately
> each to herself
>   I partake also
>   . . separately (CWP2, 246)

It is like a slow-motion way of formally vindicating the bolder pairings that Williams could once so nimbly affect in a poem like "To an Old Jaundiced Woman." Now he must more agedly hold on to the word "life" as if it were the lifeline ("no life . . . to a life, a life . . . to live") that, as in "The Desert Music," lets him connect those forward-pressing "to's" with a "two and two" alignment: "*two* woman agonize: / *to* live and *to* breathe" (as repetition slows the voice even more, demanding a meditative space between words in considering the agony of "Two—young—women"). It is the sedate maneuvering inside a sentence and scent ("The box odor . . .") which lets Williams balance himself "separately" yet nearer the women: a bodiless, airy closeness where the "*Two*" and his desiring "*to's*" come together as "Two young women / to be snared, / odor of box, / to bind and hold them / for the mind's labors." He can even go on to claim a special grasp:

> It is a love
>> less than
>>> a young man's love but,
> like this box odor

—or triadic elasticity where he can turn back on his concession—

>> more penetrant, infinitely
>>> more penetrant,
> in that sense not to be resisted.

Doubt is thus vehemently squashed by the same adverb as in "The Rose," where Williams's once-firmer language of love sent forth a steel line which "infinitely fine, infinitely / rigid penetrates / the Milky Way." There repetition and line-cut unpredictability toughen the finiteness of "rigid" pushed against the abutting, sharpened word "penetrates." But where the emphasis falls on "*infinitely* / more penetrant," in spiritual superiority to the sexual powers of young men, it is not incisiveness one hears but the clamor of afflatus.

Loose partnering, however, is quite distinct from the tightness which one hears at the start of "The Orchestra" in the same collection. There the discordant tuning-up of musicians is paired with the noise of nature's chorus:

> The precise counterpart
>> of a cacophony of bird calls (CWP2, 250)

This may not have the verve of "Ol' Bunk's Band" (1945)—"the / slap of a bass-string" plucked out as "Pick, ping"; "the horn, the / hollow horn / long drawn out" in "h*o*rn-h*o*rn-dr*a*wn-out" acoustics—but there is the same imitative impulse in seeking a syllabic "*counterpart*" to "*calls*" by means of "*cacophony*." What follows, however, is the yearning for a grand unity which will ultimately absorb all dissonance: not a cacophonous human art matching bird calls (and all that is beyond the self in the external world) but the poet-orchestra, in *Paterson*-style assertion, lifting

<pre>
                          the sun almighty
     into his sphere: wood winds
                clarinet and violins
                     sound a prolonged A!
     Ah! the sun, the sun! is about to rise
          and shed his beams
                     as he has always done
     upon us all
</pre>

Though individually entered "*into*" by the voice, "wood w*in*ds / clar*in*et and viol*ins*" yield to the wide-vowelled surge of "A!" and "Ah!": the sunrise spread out, like the over-elasticized parts of the sentence, with beating insistence in "the s*un*, the s*un*! . . . always d*one* . . . up*on*." More exultations ("Ah, ah, and ah!") make up the swelling notes, "together, unattuned / seeking a common tone": the words "*together*, un*attuned*" not yet fitting that "*tone*" until Williams declares that "Love is that common tone" and goes on to embrace, Whitman-style, all the multifarious parts of humanity's orchestra, from drudges to the sick and the dead. Thus "in spite of the / 'wrong note'" or any awkwardness that might spoil the grand harmony, the way is open for the voice to din out an unthinking, bittersweet gladness: "Repeat and repeat again . . . Repeat the theme . . . until thought / is dissolved in tears." Williams is therefore ready for the garrulous supplications of "Asphodel, That Greeny Flower" in *Journey to Love* (1955): "the love of love, / the love that swallows up all else / a grateful love, / a love of nature, of people, / animals," complementing "the Holy Light of love / that rules / blocking despair" in "The Mental Hospital Garden" (*The Desert Music*).

Yet three-ply spread is not necessarily the home of diffuse feeling and the lingered-out sentence. Form in the *Journey to Love* poem "The Pink Locust" is also the bastion of a plant's grip and a more tenacious emotional hold:

<pre>
     Tear it from the ground,
               if one hair-thin rootlet
     remain
          it will come again. (CWP2, 299)
</pre>

But it only does so "again" on the lengthening verse-line, because it can, for a short, visual moment, with vocal insistence, "remain": the minute exemplar of the careful, meditated phrasing which the layout now invites. Enlarged page-space is equally the way to the sharp, considered brevities of "The Ivy Crown" (*Journey to Love*). The crown of marriage has its thorns tautly acknowledged when Williams declares:

<pre>
     Keep
          the briars out,
</pre>

they say.
                You cannot live
                        and keep free of
briars. (CWP2, 287)

—the abrupt divisions catching the intonational punch of "out," "live," and "briars." As in the same collection's "The Drunk and the Sailor," the "wrong note" of frustrations, rather than easy harmony, comes to the fore—a staccato bark of thwartedness in

The petty fury
        that disrupts my life—
                at the striking of a wrong key (CWP2, 305)

Here Williams feels kinship with a man "about my own age / seventy": a drunk in a bus station whose cries are rendered in tense, triadic bursts: "The nerve-tingling screeches / that sprang / *sforzando.*" But the tight-clenched energy appearing there—evidence still of a surviving, unsentimental power—is locked inside an over-flaccid form or body. Though the old fisherman on the bowl of ivywood in Williams's version of Theocritus's "Idyl I" (*The Desert Music*) "poises a great net / for the cast"—

                fishing
with the full strength of his limbs
        so big do his muscles stand out
                about the neck (CWP2, 268)

—the effect here is of a sentence stretching forward and over-distributed across the page, lacking the concise ability to make the poetic muscles work for the will. Though "all the deformities take wing" in "Tribute to the Painters" (excerpted from *Paterson IV* in *Journey to Love*) the partly crippled yet battling poet has closer affinity in "The Yellow Flower" (*The Desert Music*) with Michelangelo's carving of the rebellious slave who, with his arms tied behind his back, thrusts out his torso. But, straining forward, Williams's elongated sentence shows the over-voluminous toils in which it is caught:

        I have eyes
                that are made to see and if
they see ruin for myself
        and all that I hold
                dear, they see
also
        through the eyes
                and through the lips
and tongue the power

> to free myself
> and speak of it, as
> Michelangelo through his hands
> had the same, if greater,
> power. (CWP2, 257)

Under the mufflings and flattenings imposed on statement by visuality—by the spacious layout and the poet's eyes "made to see," then laboriously "to see ruin," then to "see / also" a power—a vocal force strives to exert its contoured distinctions. Through the elastic envelope, the emphases keep pushing (*also . . . eyes . . . lips . . . tongue . . . free . . . speak*) only for the sound of speech itself to stay tamed in sameness, as Williams balances his "through's" with that of Michelangelo's—"through his hands" with "the same, if greater" (but limply revered) "power." This indeed is freedom in bondage.

By contrast, Moore at the same time (mid-1950s) can seem an unfaltering virtuoso. No circuitous struggle hinders the public-friendly voice of poetry that deals in such subjects as a concert for orphans, a televised opera, a race horse, baseball players, an old amusement park, the rescue of Carnegie Hall, or the dazzle of the flamenco dancer Soledad in "Style" (1956). The latter poem's acoustic flash of images could even make it appear that Moore is here rivaling Williams's ability to keep pace with a performance in "Ol' Bunk's Band." But where he adheres to the body's fast compulsion ("Choking, choking! while the / treble reed / races") she deals in the rapid spirit of a dancer seemingly untrammeled by the physicality she moves into and out of:

> should we call her
> *la lagarta*? or bamboos with fireflies a-glitter;
> or glassy lake and the whorls which a vertical stroke brought about,
> of the paddle half-turned coming out.
> As if bisecting
> a viper, she can dart down three times and recover
> without a disaster, having
> been a bull-fighter. Well; she has a forgiver. (PMM, 291)

Word-facets gleam with a speedy reading that makes the lizard-like Soledad or "lag*arta*" comparable to "fire-flies a-*glitter*" or "*glassy* lake" (with "*lake*" glancing off "*lag*arta"). With a larger breath, the "wh*or*ls" of fast-flared skirts "brought ab*out*" by her stamped-down feet equally parallel the "half-turned" paddle and line which, with a twist, is finally coming "*out*." In extricating ease she can dart down as if on a "*viper*" but "rec*over*" from "disast*er*" (rhymes becoming emollient) because she has been a "bullfigh*ter*." Chiming a nonchalant pardon for that last profession ("Well; she has a forgiv*er*") is as simple for Moore as moving from a guitarist's "wrist-rest" pause, in "w*rist-rest*" tension,

to the "hand / that's suddenly set humming fast fast fast and"—a final burst—
"faster."

But none of this dexterity or wordplay glitter is driven by the inner need that
once made her speak her way, with idiosyncratic precision, through a world of
concrete particularities. Williams, on the other hand, despite the frustrations
of age, is still in touch with the urgency that forces the words, in patience and
excitement, "slow and quick," out of their creative lair, ready to strike with exactness. Three-ply may be too expansive a hiding place, but when he uses it to
catch the movement of a dancer in "The Artist" (*The Desert Music*) he reveals,
by contrast to the Moore of "Style," the compulsion which the form has kept
safe. What might seem an over-leisurely submission of the voice to a visually
partitioned sentence, demanding pauses at predictable points—as Mr. T.

>   stood on his toes
>   heels together
>   arms gracefully
>   for the moment
>   curled above his head

—is actually a preparation for the compressive zest which follows:

>   Then he whirled about
>   bounded
>   into the air
>   and with an *entrechat*
>   perfectly achieved
>   completed the figure.

Word against word, "whirled a*bout*" sends forth "b*ou*nded" "*into* the air" and
"an *entrechat*": the brief suspense of feet crisscrossed above the ground and
seen-spoken in clinching delight ("an entre*chat* / perfectly a*chi*eved"). While
the dancer in Moore's "Arthur Mitchell" (1962) eludes sight by his minimal
embodiment ("Slim dragonfly / too rapid for the eye / to cage") Mr. T. gives
airborne value back to physicality—Williams using triadic space unloosely to
complete the "figure" of a design on the page and in sound.

He keeps hold of a pressure that has not been lost, despite the lingerings
of the boxwood odor in "Daphne and Virginia" or the "sweet-scented" flower
of the imagination in "Asphodel." Indeed the aroma-less quality of language,
unladen by old yearnings, which he had always admired in Moore—words
held together in taut apposition, without a gluing obviousness—is still there
for him when he largely abandons triadic layouts in 1959 and creates new, terse
stanzas. Vocal-visual tension is central again, but now with an extra enjambed
tightness and unpunctuated starkness, suggesting how much he has swung
away from three-ply redundancies. The extended over-stretch of statement in

the passage from "The Yellow Flower" has been left behind when, in "Bird" (1959), the article-less

> Bird with outstretched
> wings poised
> inviolate unreaching
>
> yet reaching
> your image this November
> planes
>
> to a stop
> miraculously fixed in my
> arresting eyes (CWP2, 414)

But short-line arrest of vocal motion is there from the start—"poised" holding back the vowel-wide flight of "o-u-tstretched / w-i-ings," just as "*un*reaching," lineally compressed against "*in*violate" and needing a slight pause to distinguish it, pulls against the spoken sentence without stopping the onwardness. For, after the stanza-gap, "*reaching*"—emphatically distinguished in its own turn from its negative opposite—shows the vocal thrust of this stilled-yet-moving birdflight intensified: a "reaching / your" (the creature's) "image this November" as it (the verb no longer held back) all the more vigorously "*planes*" after the delay onto its watery reflection. That it "planes / to a stop," however, only completes what the regulatory breakages of line and stanza maintain to the end: the poise of energized words keeping the balance between bird and observer, as the "inviolate," independent creature planes to a halt, yet is "miraculously fixed in"—mirrored perfectly, not fixedly controlled by—the "arresting eyes" of poet and art.

Unprecipitate disclosure, with piece-by-piece surprises, is indeed an indication that Williams has once more learned to walk in verse. The 1959 poem "Chloe" (included in the group entitled "Some Simple Measures in the American Idiom and the Variable Foot") demonstrates, for example, how he measures (but with a two-and-two sense of measuring-up to) the movement of actual feet on the ground. Thus the self-conscious, adolescent Chloe is

> idly

—the word isolated in pseudo-casualness—

> tilting her weight
> from one foot
>
> to the other
> shifting

to avoid looking at me

on my way to
mail a letter
smiling to a friend (CWP2, 421)

Up goes the drawn-out lightness of "i-i-dly / tilting," while "her weight" presses down, a three-word ascent ("from one foot") balanced by a three-word fall
("to the other"). With "shifting" singled out so deliberately on its single line
(but like "idly" not halting the voice in a scripted three-ply way) Williams pinpoints the distinctly interested manner by which Chloe, with ostentation, displays *no* interest. Thus "shifting / to avoid looking at me" she keeps feignedly
aloof from the *m*-style mereness of "*me* // on *my* way to / *m*ail a letter": able to
observe the male and his *mail* while she remains, with extra-wide blitheness,
"s*m-i-l*ing to a friend." It is not the "tentative smile" of the young girl we see in
the 1960 "Elaine," but this granddaughter on the edge of womanhood, "poised
for the leap she / is not yet ready for," also has the hovering step to which Williams's new verse is especially alert,

her bare toes
starting over the clipt
lawn where she may

not go (CWP2, 396)

Ready with disobedience (the "bare t*oes* / starting *over*" lawn and clipped-
off line-end, "where she may // not"—but in word-by-word tiptoe, over the
stanza-space, does so nearly "*go*") she keeps her poise with

the tentative smile
for the adult plans laid
to trap her

calves beginning to flex
wrists
set for the getaway

So, athletically tensing against capture, "wrists" are tautly "*set*" after "*flex*" for
the greater sound of "GETaway"!

Words are also winged for takeoff, yet keep relation to ground and physicality. Rocking back and forth on the word-unit as if it were the body's un-
metrical foot—"toe and heel // heel and toe"—Williams can declare, after the
first man in space, Yuri Gagarin, has come back to earth ("Heel and Toe to
the End," 1961), that "*he*," so springy on those "*heels*," "felt / as if *he* had / been
dancing." "Sound," in Ihde's words, "dances timefully with experience"[4] as

the voice's nimble steps, kept accurate by short-line trimness, celebrate another return from flight and earthly bounty in "Landscape with the Fall of Icarus" (*Pictures from Brueghel*, 1962). Downfall would recommend a town of eight stranded whales to Dürer in "The Steeple-Jack," but it is the "grim humor" of a different foreign artist, as in the poems "Children's Games" and "The Parable of the Blind" (each man following the other, "stick in / hand triumphant to disaster"), which is translated into a different native hardiness:

> According to Brueghel
> when Icarus fell
> it was spring
>
> a farmer was ploughing
> his field
> the whole pageantry
>
> of the year was
> awake tingling
> near
>
> the edge of the sea
> concerned
> with itself
>
> sweating in the sun
> that melted
> the wings' wax
>
> unsignificantly
> off the coast
> there was
>
> a splash quite unnoticed
> this was
> Icarus drowning (CWP2, 385)

The same Icarus painting illustrates for Auden in "Musée des Beaux Arts" an Old Master's supposed reduction of large or tragic events to the merely commonplace: "how everything turns away / Quite leisurely from the disaster." But Williams, whose "splash quite unnoticed" reflects Auden, takes from Brueghel the distinctly opposite sense of a working, burgeoning world. Energy's monosyllables—"it was spring" (all the more direct after the first lines' narrative, rhymed length)—set going the impetus which is continued and expanded by the *was* of "a farmer was ploughing." Yet, with the visual cut-back of the tercet in the midst of expansion—

> his field   ploughing

—Williams keeps the quiet yet mounting delight of the spoken voice, and an even greater *was*, unextravagantly on course. It is the incision that breaks into the start of the poem's most exuberantly lengthy sentence with a stanza-dividing space—

> the whole pageantry
>
> of the year was
> awake . . .

—yet equally jams "tingling" against "awake" on the same line: no luscious overflow of spring clichés, especially not from the author of "By the Road to the Contagious Hospital," but the precise, "tingling" excitement of word propelling word in the wakeful closeness that the text's divisions visually maintain. So, "tingling / near"—with adjacency's word-sharp neighborship at "the edge of the sea" ensured by the preceding stanza-cut—the "whole pageantry // of the year" undiffusely and rhymingly runs on with the joyous voice. It is the non-royal medieval "pageantry" of unexpected contiguities—the physical suddenness of "sweating in the sun" textually separate from "concerned / with itself," yet now forcefully joining the great array—where the laborers who sweat under that sun and the aviator whose wings' wax is melted by its heat become unexpected neighbors. For as the vocal impetus continues, this is a single world made whole out of breakings-off—a sentence ended, yet the penultimate sentence carrying on the exultance which makes "*un*significantly off the coast" so significant in emphasis. What stands out and what "was // a splash quite unnoticed" has the joyous *was* which has already been heard in "was spring . . . was ploughing . . . was / awake." For "this was," it turns out—and even more positively so—"Icarus *drowning*": the vocal plunge into a self-engrossed world of energies that Williams's counter-cutting detachment makes the topmost point of the entire poem.

But, says a commentator who is against the speaking of this poem, because to utter it is to exclude (supposedly) other possibilities: "When we look at ["Landscape with the Fall of Icarus"] . . . we see that it is actually unvoicable in any completely satisfactory way: the polyvocality, the simultaneity of possible tones, rhythms, and interpretations, is available only to the inner ear, and cannot be spoken. One might therefore conclude that it is impossible to read this poem well aloud."[5] One's conclusion, however, in the final pages of this study, must be completely the opposite. For in choosing to speak Williams's poem aloud as a sequential unfolding, rather than staying silent in contemplation of alternatives—solely imaginary choices, however, which the anti-vocal viewpoint always leaves unshown and unproven—the reader not only discovers textures hidden to the deafened ear (a climactic death by water, for example, that so amazingly enlivens) but is witness once more to the poet's capacity for survival and artistic recovery.

Indeed, speaking Williams's poetry again brings us close to the separate strengths of Eliot and Moore at their finest, when set side by side as vocalists to whom we actually listen. Just as Eliot's rhythms of submergence and ascent in *The Waste Land* pinpoint the tension between engagement and extrication in the verse of *Spring and All*, so the Williams kind of interplay—as crucial as the setting of form against onward speech without Eliot's collage of allusions—heightens one's sense, by its deft surface quality, of the greater unconscious depth from which Eliot's articulation has to climb. This is his creative hiding place of strength and vulnerability where he can be prey to the sound of mechanical fatalism or, with the New England gulls of *Ash-Wednesday* and the "Quick quick quick" prompting of "Cape Ann," the surpassor of deadliness. Therefore if one puts Williams's Icarus poem alongside another poetic death by water—the lines on a drowned Phoenician sailor in *The Waste Land*—one becomes more auditorily alert, on the verse-swell, to an undersea resurgence breaking through. Stultified consciousness is being reached beyond when Phlebas leaves behind his mercantile calculations of "profit and loss":

> A current under sea
> Picked his bones in whispers. As he rose and fell
> He passed the stages of his age and youth
> Entering the whirlpool.
>   Gentile or Jew
> O you who turn the wheel and look to windward,
> Consider Phlebas, who was once handsome and tall as you. (CPP, 71)

Significantly the sailor first appeared as a figure of escape at the end of the French-language poem "Dans Le Restaurant" (1917) after a waiter has told his tale of a rainy day in childhood, his tickling of a young girl to make her laugh, and how he was scared off by "un gros chien." Reacting against the story, as if it expressed too openly his own remembered failures and sexual fears, an outraged customer gives the waiter ten sous to cleanse himself in the public baths—all a pretext for the poem's extraordinary leap to the final stanza about the drowned Phlebas, now washed free of his past in a greater bath.[6] But while the French of "Dans Le Restaurant" seems Eliot's way of taking refuge from an over-naked expression of painful thoughts, his translation of the Phlebas stanza and its notable revision in *The Waste Land*—a foreign-sharpened English, as throughout the poem—distinctly spurs on the flight from the moribund. So, though Phlebas, the significantly *non*-American sailor,[7] suffers "un sort pénible" (or "a painful fate") in the original, as "A current undersea bore him away, deep down" ("Un courant de sous-mer l'emporta tres loin") the English vowels of a "*current under sea*" suggest an un-elegiac stirring: the vowel-assiduous quiet of "*Picked his bones in whispers*" that characteristically leads Eliot from a non-grandiose sound to an earned and louder vitality—beyond "the st*ages*" of Phlebas's "*age* and youth" (English assonance going beyond the lingered-on "étapes" of his "vie antérieure") to the new feature of "Entering the whirlpool." For this is not, when spoken, a plunge into a Poe-like maelstrom or automatism, but the upward step, in the rise-fall swell of "*Entering the whirlpool*," that resounds in "*Gentile or Jew*" as the open vowels spaciously lead out from "*Jew*" to "*you who . . . look to windward*." It is the ascent of tone completely overriding the memento mori idea, now that the voice advancing from "*whirlpool*" to "*wheel*" and "*windward*" leaves behind any sense of time's barren round and boldly hails the voyager, "handsome and tall," turning that wheel with live command.

Reaching out so directly brings an essential reminder of the starting-point that Eliot shares with Moore and Williams as a poet of the spoken voice. But the acoustic shifts by which Eliot-Ferdinand at the end of *The Waste Land* stretches from nursery rhyme, Dantean fire, and *Pervigilium Veneris* to a Tennysonian bird ("O swallow swallow")—the multi-tongued searchings that provoke Williams to arraign him with "THE TRADITIONALISTS OF PLAGIARISM"[8]—bring him closer to Moore's art. She, with her tension of secrecy-yet-revelation ("Openly, yes"; but form-bound in guardedness, whether in the undersea lair of "The Fish" or with the frigate pelican's Handel-like hidden power) has the cultural sympathy which sets her apart from Williams's assertions of the "American idiom"[9] and which makes her, in the 1923 "Novices," for example, a partial imitator of Eliot, with another death by water. While history's force assaults the deadened mind in "Gerontion" ("De Bailhache, Fresca, Mrs. Cammel, whirled . . . in fractured atoms") a linguistic ocean (antiquity's "tempestuous energy" and the Hebrew language) sweeps away a callowness toward the past and "the little assumptions of the scared ego" as it breaks on shore

> with its "great livid stains like long slabs of green marble,"
> its "flashing lances of perpendicular lightning" and "molten fires
>   swallowed up,"
> "with foam on its barriers,"
> "crashing itself out in one long hiss of spray." (OB, 71)

Yet, controlling the breath and holding up the bulk of so much seemingly un-edited quotation, without letting it fall before the final "hiss of spray," suggests to a speaker of the poem how very clearly Moore has gone her own independent way. Whatever the *Waste Land*-style notes for the quotations at the end of the 1924 *Observations*, where the poem first appeared (the volume's title itself respectful of *Prufrock and Other Observations*), whatever, indeed, her acknowledgments to *The Expositor's Bible* for the final and penultimate lines, to Leigh Hunt for "molten fires" and Flaubert for "long slabs," her quotations strike the ear not as Eliot-like fusions of new wholes out of fragments but like the Inca masonry, edge to edge without obvious cement, that Williams admired. Vocally holding the blocks together, yet keeping them visually apart with quotation marks, she once more shows the kind of regulatory grip that Williams could learn from. His voice-sight friction in his best short-line verse has its equivalent in her traversing of knots, meticulous discriminations, and heaped-up barriers, beginning with early rhymed tercets, then moving on to the stranger configurations of syllable-counted grids and free verse—the impediments fought through, made sayably difficult even, in keeping true to the mind's quirky idiom.

For Moore the resister, it is also a matter of saying no again and again so as to define the exact ground one can dwell in. What Williams's English grandmother battles for in his "Dedication" ("against . . . against . . . against") has to be achieved in Moore's "New York" (1921) by her vehemently winnowing away what she will *not* have of this country: "not the dime-novel exterior . . . not the atmosphere of ingenuity . . . not the plunder" but finally (quoting from James)[10] the "accessibility to experience"—the small, positive aperture opened at last onto a civil yet invigorating American ground. She is there the poet of "The Steeple-Jack" and "Virginia Britannia," commanding a middle position between Eliot and Williams; nearer indeed the latter than the former, as regards the native scene, but with the moderation that sanely refuses to go to Williams's extremes when he wars against expatriate Eliot. Her Anglophilia aids judgment. For what one can see as valuable in Williams's affirmation of the "local," when he radiates its significance outward with unexorbitant mastery—and when his feeling for the concrete here-and-now challenges Eliot's denigrations in *Ash-Wednesday*—equally lets one observe the prejudicial narrowness that batters against *The Waste Land*: the very poem, one notes, where his affinity with Eliot's struggle in difficult ground, and the constant re-winning of coherences out of fragmentation, is so manifest. It is ironic that Williams should start to praise Eliot in the 1940s for what he perceives as the other's new localism[11] at the very time, "the waste sad time," when Eliot's more dislocated spirit occupies the English places of *Four Quartets*.

Yet one's final thought is not what falls away but what endures, and Williams's contribution is indispensable. He, whose shaping power survived the longest of the three poets, can here serve to represent them by the kind of poem they would never write, but which exemplifies, at their best, their own undefeated persistence. In "The Wind Increases" (1930) he rides with the blast as

>   The trees
>   the tulip's bright
>   tips
>   sidle and
>   toss— (CWP2, 339)

Now it is not short-line tightness but the wind-like thrust of words across the page's airy spaces which keeps spoken language on its mettle. A sentence started and scattered to the right—"The trees"—must be re-begun with extra stubbornness from the left, when, following "*trees*," "the *tulip's* brigh*t* / *tips*" assert their sharp edges, and "*tips*" hovers in vocal-visual alignment with "*tu-lip's*." Though "sidle" tugs against such poise, "*toss*" pulls it back again, kicking off the next word, "L*oose*" ("Loose your love / to flow // Blow!")—not with am-orous vapidity, however, but with a cry of exact and purposeful feeling from

>   a man
>   whose words will
>   bite
>   their way
>
>   home—

Striving against the rightward outfling, these spoken words "bite / their way / *home*" with the clenched pressure by which language,

>   gripping
>   the ground

cleaves to substance, whether native soil or energy's axis. What Moore and Eliot individually know as words' excited fidelity, Williams, "*gripping* // the *g*round," knows in tenacious tracking as

>   a way
>   to the last leaftip

—a route again in "leaftip" smallness to multifoliate branching, a means once more by which the speaking voice accurately accompanies—indeed marries—the greater sounded world.

NOTES

Introduction

1. Williams, "The Poem" in *The Wedge*; Eliot, *The Use of Poetry and the Use of Criticism*, 119; Moore, quoting from Williams's "April" in her May 1934 *Poetry* review of his *Collected Poems 1921–1931*, reprinted in *The Complete Prose of Marianne Moore*, 325; Moore, reviewing Eliot's *The Sacred Wood* in the March 1921 *Dial*, reprinted in *Complete Prose*, 55.

2. Pound, letter to Marianne Moore, 16 December 1918, printed in *The Selected Letters of Ezra Pound: 1907–1941*, 143.

3. Baker, *Modernism and the Harlem Renaissance*, 106, 47.

4. Schweighauser, *The Noises of American Literature, 1890–1985*, 90.

5. The trajectory of discussion leads, among others, from Charles Olson's essay on Projective Verse in 1950 to the diversity of approaches in Charles Bernstein's 1998 anthology *Close Listening*, Jonathan Rée on the philosophy of sound in *I See a Voice* (1999), Steven Connor's historical investigations of acoustics and ventriloquy in *Dumbstruck* (2001), John Picker on Dickens and George Eliot in *Victorian Soundscapes* (2003), and the work on twentieth-century avant-garde acoustics in *The Poetry of Sound/The Sound of Poetry* (2009) edited by Marjorie Perloff and Craig Dworkin.

6. Sayre, *The Visual Text of William Carlos Williams*.

7. Cushman, *William Carlos Williams and the Meaning of Measure*, 47–48.

8. *The Selected Letters of William Carlos Williams*, ed. John Thirlwall, 50.

9. Sound is again made subordinate to the "visual phrase" by George W. Layng, "Rephrasing Whitman, Williams and the Visual Idiom," 183.

10. Ong, *Orality and Literacy*, 119.

11. Ihde, *Listening and Voice*, 11.

12. *William Carlos Williams: The Collected Recordings* (Keele, 1992, 1993). Republished online by PennSound (University of Pennsylvania) 2007.

13. Griffiths, *The Printed Voice of Victorian Poetry*, 17.

14. Olson, *Projective Verse*, 22.

15. Pound, letter to Hubert Creekmore, February 1939, printed in *Selected Letters*, 322.

16. Levy, "Natural Reticence: Editing Marianne Moore," 237.

17. Miller, *The Linguistic Moment: From Wordsworth to Stevens*, 362, 363. "[T]he red wheelbarrow, the locust tree in flower, the young sycamore . . . stand fixed in their poems, on the page, in the span of an instant" (361).

18. When first published in *Dial* 82 (March 1927).

19. Eliot, review of Moore's *Poems* and *Marriage*: "Miss Moore works the uneasy language of stereotypes—as of a whole people playing uncomfortably at clenches and clevelandisms—with impeccable skill into her pattern."

CHAPTER ONE   Voices of a Common Ground

1. Eliot, "Reflections on Contemporary Poetry," 40: "[Conrad] Aiken . . . does not escape his fatal American introspectiveness. . . . He is tangled in himself . . . if he was in contact with European civilisation, he might go so very much further."

2. Eliot, "Mr. Lee Masters," review of *Songs and Satires* by Edgar Lee Masters.

3. Williams, "Tract," 139ff.

4. Ihde, *Listening and Voice*, 168.

5. Williams, *Kora in Hell: Improvisations*, in *Imaginations*, 14.

6. Eliot, "'Rhetoric' and Poetic Drama" (1919), reprinted in *Selected Essays*, 41.

7. In praising the "living and terrible force" of the speech by Sylla's ghost in *Catiline* ("Ben Jonson," *Selected Essays*, 150), Eliot observes that it "does . . . not overflow the outline." Reviewing *Donne's Sermons*, he also found that confines could be crammed to bursting because Donne "had more in him than could be squeezed into the frame of this form: something which, if it does not crack the frame, at least gives it now and then, a perceptible bulge" ("The Preacher as Artist").

8. See also Marjorie Perloff on this passage in *21st Century Modernism*, 20.

9. "Vocalism" had an acoustic influence on another Eliot (George), as John M. Picker notes in *Victorian Soundscapes*. Whitman supplies the epigraph to chapter 29 of Eliot's *Daniel Deronda* in which Gwendolen hears, as a contrast to her husband's "toneless drawl," Deronda's voice, like "the deep notes of a violoncello":

Surely whoever speaks to me in the right voice, him or her shall I follow,
As the water follows the moon, silently, with fluid steps, anywhere around the globe.
(371)

10. Williams, prologue to *Kora in Hell* in *Imaginations*, 24. Jepson's claim appears in "The Western School," 9.

11. Williams, *In the American Grain*, 35.

12. Eliot, letter to Herbert Read, 23 April 1928, quoted in *T. S. Eliot: The Man and His Work*, ed. Allen Tate, 15.

13. Williams, *Yes, Mrs. Williams*, 28.

14. Pound, letter to Williams, 10 November 1917, printed in *Selected Letters*, 123–124.

15. Williams, *The Autobiography of William Carlos Williams*, 60.

16. Williams, recording for the Library of Congress, 5 May 1945, *Collected Recordings*.

17. Williams, "Sample Prose Piece: The Three Letters," 11.

18. Sheldon, *Salvation Nell*, reprinted in *Best Plays of the Early American Theatre*, ed. John Gassner, 557–616. The play begins on "A bitterly cold Christmas Eve" in a New York bar where Nell, also vainly, urges her own drunken Jim to return home.

19. This is to differ from Rod Townley who "suspects" that Williams "saw the play in the poem" (*The Early Poetry of William Carlos Williams*, 89–90).

20. Notably as recorded for Richard Wirtz Emerson at Rutherford, August 1950 (*Collected Recordings*).

21. Moore, interviewed in the broadcast series "The Poet Speaks" (c. 1951, radio station unknown), Yale Historical Recordings Collection.

22. Moore, talking to Grace Schulman, "A Conversation with Marianne Moore," 158. Moore speaks lines from her early poem "I May, I Might, I Must," and says: "There, ev-

erything comes in straight order, just as if I had not thought it before, and were talking to you. Unstrained and natural."

23. Smith, *The Acoustic World of Early Modern England*, 129.

24. Writing a note for a reading at the Guggenheim Museum in 1950, Williams recalled how Eliot had said, when they met at the Library of Congress in November 1948: "Williams[,] you've given us some good characters in your work, let's have more of them." Quoted by Paul Mariani, *William Carlos Williams*, 831.

CHAPTER TWO   To Hew Form Truly

1. The Bryn Mawr *Lantern* 23 (spring 1915).

2. Disraelian variety, as acted on American stages by George Arliss in a 1911–1914 touring production of Louis N. Parker's *Disraeli*, may well have impressed Moore, as it certainly did Willa Cather, who noted the "quicksilver fancy" of Arliss's performance ("New Types of Acting," 42).

3. More, "Disraeli and Conservatism," reprinted in *Shelburne Essays*, 185, 160. Moore's review of André Maurois's *Disraeli: A Picture of the Victorian Age* (*Dial* 84, May 1928, 435, 437; reprinted in *Complete Prose*, 255–256) shows that she also knew biographical work on Disraeli by Gladstone, Peel, and Derby.

4. Craig, describing the illustration of Antony in the forum scene that faces page 104, *On the Art of the Theatre*.

5. Craig, preface to *Towards a New Theatre*, 2.

6. *Egoist* 4.2, April 1915, 62.

7. Ellen Levy's point in "Natural Reticence: Editing Marianne Moore," 237: Moore struggled to establish "a place for herself in a cultural battleground."

8. Baxter, *The Saint's Everlasting Rest*, vol. 1, 265.

9. Ibid., 248.

10. Ibid., 343 (vol. 2); 299 (vol. 1); 266 (vol. 1); 343 (vol. 2).

11. "In This Age of Hard Trying, Nonchalance is Good and," first publication of the poem in *Chimaera* 1.2, July 1916, 52–53.

12. The Bryn Mawr *Lantern* (Spring 1917), 50–51.

13. *Egoist* 5.4 (April 1918), 55–56.

14. Moore's admiration for poems in *Satires of Circumstance* ("Outside the Window," "A Thunderstorm," and "The Abbey Mason," for instance) is shown by her 1920 essay "English Literature since 1914."

15. Emerson, "Sea-Shore," in *The Works of Ralph Waldo Emerson: Poems*:

I heard or seemed to hear the chiding Sea
Say, Pilgrim . . .

. . . .

I make your sculptured architecture vain,
Vain beside mine. I drive my wedges home.
And carve the coastwise mountain into caves.

16. Contrary to the scholarship which has more recently awarded *The Revenger's Tragedy* to Thomas Middleton, I believe that its maniacally taut style, and its inimitable skeletal humor, still belong to Cyril Tourneur or another non-Middletonian dramatist.

17. A language without "any definite meaning, a transrational language": the Futurist aim of Alexander Kruchenykh, as quoted by Nancy Perloff in "Sound Poetry and the Musical Avant-Garde: A Musicologist's Perspective," 101.

18. "Bruitism," a Dadaist noise music, was a term coined by Richard Huelsenbeck in the spirit of Marinetti: see Douglas Kahn, *Noise, Water, Meat: A History of Sound in the Arts*, 45-46.

19. Hugo Ball's "verse without words," says Steve McCaffery, "is testimony to the omnipresent possibility, in cacophony and gibberish, of language returning in either recognizable words or a comprehensible 'syntax' suggestive of an unknown language" ("Voice in Extremis," 164). François Dufrêne, an "Ultralettriste" of the 1950s, allegedly "exploded language in order to unleash the possibilities of a new language": as quoted from Joao Fernandes by Nancy Perloff, "Sound Poetry and the Musical Avant-Garde: A Musicologist's Perspective," 115.

20. Unsigned editorial introducing "Those Various Scalpels" and "In the Days of Prismatic Color" (originally spelled "Colour" when it appeared in the Bryn Mawr *Lantern* 27, spring 1919), *Contact* 2 (January 1921), 2. Though Robin Schulze assigns it to Williams's fellow-editor, Robert McAlmon (*Becoming Marianne Moore: The Early Poems, 1907-1924*, 413), I suggest that it is the criticism of a "windy prairie" style in the Whitman-Sandburg vein from an "analytic" (and poet's) standpoint which decisively marks the editorial as Williams's.

21. Pound, letter to Williams, 10 November 1917, printed in *Selected Letters*, 124.

22. Williams, "Belly Music," 28.

23. Williams, "By the road to the contagious hospital," 208.

24. Henry James, addressing a graduating class at Bryn Mawr, 8 June 1905, before Moore's arrival as a student, speaks of "the innumerable, differentiated, discriminated units of sound and sense that lend themselves to audible production, to enunciation, to intonation" (*The Question of our Speech / The Lesson of Balzac*, 20).

25. Williams, *The Collected Poems of William Carlos Williams I, 1909-1939*, 231.

26. Williams, *In the American Grain*, 213.

27. Eliot, "American Literature," 23.

CHAPTER THREE   Sounding *The Waste Land*

1. Walker, *The Transparent Lyric*, 13.

2. Perloff, *The Poetics of Indeterminacy*, 162.

3. Eliot, recording of *The Waste Land*, 26 July 1946, at the NBC studios, New York, for the Library of Congress, published by the Library and HarperAudio.

4. "He sang it & chanted it[,] rhythmed it. It has great beauty & force of phrase: symmetry; & tensity": entry for 23 June 1922, *The Diary of Virginia Woolf II, 1920-1924*, ed. A.O. Bell, 178.

5. Eliot recorded *The Waste Land* in the studio at Columbia University run by William Cabell Greet, professor of English at Barnard College, and his colleague, George Hibbitt. The studio had originally been set up for the recording of American dialects, but Greet also used it for the recording of poets. Vachel Lindsay recorded a large number of poems here in January 1931, and in May 1933 Eliot recorded *Ash-Wednesday* and other verse. The Columbia library catalogue dates his recording of *The Waste Land* as 1935 (a

date that I followed when writing my article, "Sounding *The Waste Land*: T. S. Eliot's 1935 recording," *P.N. Review* 28.1, September–October 2001, 54–61). But it is now clear that Eliot was not in the United States that year, and the more likely date (May 1933, the same as Eliot's other recordings at Columbia) is suggested by the *Barnard Bulletin* (16 February 1934, 3) which reports Greet's lecture on Alumnae Day four days previously when, among various recordings, he played "part of T. S. Eliot's 'Waste Land.'" The recording was published online by Poetry Archive, UK, in 2007 and by Faber and Faber and Touch Press as an iPad app in 2011.

6. Baudelaire: "Ce sinistre vieillard qui se multiplait."

7. The acoustic assault on Stetson is heightened by its being made against the fashionable façade implied by his very name. John B. Stetson and Company claim in an illustrated advertisement (*Vanity Fair*, February 1921, 5) that "When the English speak of 'swagger,' they mean that touch of trig, easy smartness, so marked in the very fit Stetson model."

8. As changed from Cornelia's song in John Webster, *The White Devil*, V.iv:

But keepe the wolfe far thence, that's foe to men,
For with his nailes, hee'l dig them up agen.

9. In both recordings, 1933 and 1946, Eliot changes "behind his wing" to "beneath his wing," and therefore makes the parenthetic burden heavier as it weighs down the urge to rise.

10. See Martin Peerson, *Private Musick, Or the First Book of Ayres and Dialogues* (1620) XVII, in E. H. Fellowes, *English Madrigal Verse 1588-1632*, 164:

But O, hark how the birds sing, mark that note,
Jug, jug, tereu, tereu,
Prettily warbled from a sweet throat.

11. When played on the piano, the language of the 1912 song (lyric by Gene Buck and Herman Ruby; music by David Stamper) clearly has no Eliotic abruptness. Instead there is a rolling ease in

That Shakespearean rag,—
Most intelligent, very elegant,
That old classical drag

12. For an account of Eliot's treatment at Lausanne in late 1921 under the direction of Roger Vittoz, see Cleo McNelly Kearns, *T. S. Eliot and Indic Traditions*, 152–157.

13. "In the opera, these voices of boys impinge on the deep masculinity of the singing of the Knights of the Grail—and Verlaine's line beautifully recreates the surprise and purity of that Wagnerian moment in his own sonnet" (Charles Tomlinson, *Poetry and Metamorphosis* (1981 Clark Lectures), in *Metamorphoses: Poetry and Translation*, 134).

14. Ibid., 125. "Eliot's note points us to Wagner's *Götterdämmerung*, Act III, Scene I, where the Rhine-maidens address Siegfried.... But what they in fact don't do in Act III of *Götterdämmerung* is to sing their 'Weialala leia / Wallala leialala.' They begin in Act III by lamenting that the Rhine is now dark because their gold has been stolen.... 'Weialala' etc. is the joyful noise that *opens* the *Ring* cycle in *Das Rheingold*, before the theft of the gold."

15. See also "What the Rattlesnake Said," "What the Coal-Heaver Said," "What the

Snow Man Said," and other titles in the section "Moon Poems," originally published in *The Congo and Other Poems*.

16. Eliot's French bird and "flash of lightning" speedily recall Edmond Rostand's cock (the artistic imagination) in his verse-play *Chantecler*, "stretching out his song as if to hoist up the sun" (*"allongéant son chant comme pour haler le soleil"*). Crying at last "Cocorico!" Chantecler staggers back with his beloved Pheasant-hen, both "suddenly flooded with light" (*"inondés brusquement de lumière"*), 119.

17. "'Boy!' False hound . . . I / Fluttered your Volscians in Corioles. / Alone I did it. 'Boy!'" (Shakespeare, *Coriolanus*, V.v).

18. Kyd, *The Spanish Tragedy*, IV.ii.

19. See the 1615 title page of *The Spanish Tragedy or Hieronimo is Mad Againe*, as reproduced in Bruce R. Smith, *The Acoustic World of Early Modern England*, 122. The scrolls of speech-parts issuing from characters' mouths in the illustration below the title, and the implicit clamor emergent from the silent page at the pictured discovery of Hieronimo's son's murder, indicate, according to Smith (129), the persistent need for a reader, even at that late date, to turn "the fixed body of type into a living, sounding thing by marking 'sentences,'" to be remembered in a commonplace book or used in conversation.

20. As in Tomlinson's recording, *Charles Tomlinson Reads* The Waste Land *by T. S. Eliot*.

21. Williams, *Autobiography*, 146. Moore retorted, "I was never a rafter holding up anyone!" when interviewed by Donald Hall in November 1960 ("Marianne Moore," 62).

22. "I was intensely jealous of this man who was much more cultured than I was": Williams interviewed by Walter Sutton, October–November 1960, *Collected Recordings*.

23. Williams, *Autobiography*, 146.

24. McAlmon, "A Vacation's Job" in *A Hasty Bunch*, 204–205.

25. Williams, "Robert McAlmon's Prose (I)," review of *A Hasty Bunch*. Following on from the comment by the student David in "A Vacation's Job"—"The only ideal that is worth possessing is that of intelligence" (178)—Williams says in his review (363): "The thing is that a life is going on, an intelligence is riding these things, searching through them. . . . Why waste time in dwelling on the unessential flood except . . . to show its impact upon the great concern, a free life of the intelligence which is entirely apart . . . riding the flood . . . ?" Williams had read *A Hasty Bunch* in late 1921, before writing most of *Spring and All*. See Sanford J. Smoller, *Adrift Among Geniuses*, 345.

CHAPTER FOUR   Riding the Flood

1. Williams, "Robert McAlmon's Prose (I)," 362.

2. Eliot, "Tradition and the Individual Talent," reprinted in *Selected Essays*, 16.

3. In "Not of Any School," Patricia C. Willis recounts how Moore read about a newly excavated Egyptian artifact ("A Fish-Shaped Bottle from Tell-Armana," as it was called in T. R. Peet's article "Home Life in Ancient Egypt 3000 Years Ago," *Illustrated London News* 15, 6 August 1921, 182–185). From this discovery originated the final version of "An Egyptian Pulled Glass Bottle in the Shape of a Fish," as discussed here in chapter 5.

4. Toomer, *Cane*, 52–53: "Life of nigger alleys, of pool rooms and restaurants and near-beer saloons soaks into the walls of Howard Theater and sets them throbbing jazz songs. . . . Girls dance and sing. The walls sing and press inward."

5. Hartley, "The Importance of Being Dada," in *Adventures in the Arts*, 253, 251.

6. Williams's changing attitude to the Dadaists is detailed in the *Spring and All* chapter of Christopher MacGowan, *William Carlos Williams's Early Poetry*.

7. Williams, "Marianne Moore" (1925), *Imaginations*, 317.

8. *Collected Poems I*, 235.

9. North, *The Dialect of Modernism*, 154–155.

10. Williams, *In the American Grain*, 209.

11. North, *The Dialect of Modernism*, 11.

12. Here I differ from Peter Halter's assumption in *The Revolution in the Visual Arts and the Poetry of William Carlos Williams* that Williams is verbally copying a specific painted plant. The poem, he says, recreates "in words many of the effects of Charles Demuth's watercolor" (85): that is, *Tuberoses*, which was bought by Williams in 1922 but which is clearly not the same—with its white flowers, dark red leaves of *Polianthes tuberosa*, three pots, and no lamp—as the pot of flowers in the poem. Working by the same visual assumption that Williams is simply copying a picture, Bram Dijkstra says in *The Hieroglyphics of a New Speech* (190–191) that "Young Sycamore" adheres "minutely to the facts of [Charles] Stieglitz's photograph," *Street View in New York City* (1902). The claim is challenged by Monique Claire Vescia in *Depression Glass*, 114–115.

13. *Collected Poems I*, 184.

14. Williams, *I Wanted to Write a Poem*, 42.

15. Williams, "Marianne Moore" (1925), *Imaginations*, 315.

16. Ibid., 319. See also William Bronk's poem "The Beautiful Well: Macchu Picchu" (*Life Supports: New and Collected Poems*) where Inca stones are praised for their "unmortared, close / accommodation, stone to different stone, / exactly interlocked."

17. Williams, "Marianne Moore" (1925), *Imaginations*, 317–318.

18. For example, in Williams's first recorded reading of the poem, 9 January 1942, for the National Council of Teachers of English, *Collected Recordings*.

19. Williams, "Marianne Moore" (1925), *Imaginations*, 317.

20. In an unpublished MA thesis ("The Paterson Metaphor in William Carlos Williams's *Paterson*," 10), Geri M. Rhodes reports being told by the director of Rutherford Public Library that Williams himself had said that he composed "The Red Wheelbarrow" "while looking out a window from the house where one of his patients, a little girl, lay suspended between life and death." My thanks to John Wheatcroft for this reference. When Williams visited Bucknell University in the 1950s, he gave Wheatcroft a similar account. Making a doctor's call on a child "gravely ill with fever," says Wheatcroft, "Williams realized the fate of the child was out of his hands. While he waited to see which way it would go, he walked to the window where outside in the rain he fixed on a red wheelbarrow." See also *An Introduction to Poetry* where X. J. Kennedy draws on Rhodes's account.

21. Shakespeare, *Richard II*, I.iii.

22. *Collected Poems I*, 234.

23. Williams, *The Great American Novel*, reprinted in *Imaginations*, 175.

24. *In the American Grain*, 130.

25. Ibid., 136.

26. Ibid., 71.

27. Ibid., 70.

28. Ibid., 234.

29. Ibid., 124.

30. Ibid., 123. The French comes from *Lettres édifiantes et curieuses concernant l'Asie, l'Afrique et l'Amérique*, ed. Louis Aimé-Martin, 678.

31. Ibid., 688, and *In the American Grain*, 127. See Bryce Conrad, *Refiguring America*, 23–24, 39–43, for a discussion of the "eating" motif in the Rasles chapter.

32. *In the American Grain*, 227.

33. Ibid., 228 and 221.

34. Ibid., 229.

35. Ibid., 221.

36. Ibid., 216. The "genius of place" clearly stems from "The Spirit of Place" chapter in D. H. Lawrence's *Studies in Classic American Literature*, first published in the United States in August 1923, just before Williams began his year-long sabbatical of research for *In the American Grain*. But it is Lawrence who is notably skeptical about Williams's choice of Poe as his great adventurer: "Does not Mr. Williams mistake Poe's agony of *destructive penetration*, through all the horrible bastard-Europe alluvium of his 1840 America, for the positive America itself?" (Review of *In the American Grain*, *Nation*, 14 April 1926, reprinted in *Phoenix: The Posthumous Papers of D. H. Lawrence*, 336).

37. *In the American Grain*, 225.

38. Eliot, "American Literature and the American Language," reprinted in *To Criticize the Critic*, 54–55.

39. *In the American Grain*, 232.

40. By 1958 Williams had moved so far from his praise of Poe as the anti-verbose stylist of method and logic that he could tell Edith Heal: "Poe was . . . a genius but too restricted in his style. . . . He existed at the center of his peculiar world. Wasn't able to get away from it; destroyed himself" (*I Wanted to Write a Poem*, 44).

41. Poe, "Our American Poets, No. I—Flaccus," reprinted in *The Complete Works of Edgar Allan Poe* vol. 12, 163.

42. Thomas Ward ("Flaccus"), *Passaic: A Group of Poems Touching That River*, quoted by Poe, *Complete Works*, 164.

43. Ibid.

44. Williams, recording of *Paterson I.iii* for the Library of Congress, 18 October 1947, *Collected Recordings*.

CHAPTER FIVE   The Animal Vernacular

1. Moore, review of *Ideas of Order* by Wallace Stevens, in *Criterion* 15 (January 1936), reprinted in *Complete Prose*, 329.

2. Slatin, *The Savage's Romance*, 36–37. His discussion shows the frustration implicit in Moore's 1917 poem "Sojourn in the Whale," where she associates herself with Ireland the year after the suppressed Easter Rising: "Trying to open locked doors with a sword, threading / The points of needles, planting shade trees / Upside down . . ."

3. Schuchard suggests in *Eliot's Dark Angel* (90–94) that Eliot's betrayal by his wife and Russell lies behind the second epigraph to the poem from the anonymous play *The Raigne of King Edward III*, II.ii, when the King compares the virtuous Countess of Salis-

bury to the music of the nightingale: "And why should I speake of the nightingale? / The nightingale sings of adulterate wrong." The lines, in capital letters, were published with the other epigraph in the February 1920 edition of *Ara Vos Prec*, but were removed before the poem appeared in the 1921 American edition.

4. Together with "Flaccus," the name of another versifier attacked by Poe makes its reappearance. See Poe, "Our Amateur Poets, No. III. William Ellery Channing [the younger]," reprinted in *Complete Works*, vol. 12, 175: "[Channing's poems] are more preposterous . . . than any poems except those of the author of 'Sam Patch' . . ."

5. Williams, reading for the Library of Congress, 5 May 1945, *Collected Recordings*.

6. Frederick Triebel's depiction of the senator in Statuary Hall shows a portly frock-coated figure with "SHOUP" in capitals on the plinth.

7. Williams, *In the American Grain*, 141.

8. Williams, "Introduction for the Composer: An Occasion for Music," in *The First President: Libretto for an Opera (and Ballet)*, reprinted in *Many Loves and Other Plays*, 303.

9. Ibid.

10. Draft of "Between Walls," Yale collection, ZA 49.

11. Recorded 19 March 1952, *Collected Recordings*.

12. Moore, letter to Williams, 7 December 1936, printed in *The Selected Letters of Marianne Moore*, 371: "The untainted finality of your reading, and things that you said, exhilarated me. . . . Miss Bishop said she felt she must now 'read all' you 'have written,' and has been giving much thought to your anti-sonnet theory of form; as I have also; we being animals, however, with a little different markings from yours." As for Bishop's memory of the occasion, "I have no recollection of anything that was read, except for a sea-monster poem of Williams's, during which he gave some loud and realistic roars" ("Efforts of Affection: A Memoir of Marianne Moore," c. 1969, 142).

13. Moore recast the lines as free verse and rephrased them with weaker effect in the 1967 *Complete Poems*:

Demonstrate on him how the lady placed a forked stick
on the innocuous neck-sides of the dangerous southern snake.
One need not try to stir him up; his prune-shaped head and
alligator-eyes are not party to the joke.

Spoken flatness succeeds the previous articulated accuracy. Now that the lady no longer has "caught" the snake, and has merely "placed" the stick on "neck-sides" (with Moore loosening the close acoustic connection between "forked stick" and "innocuous neck") the teasing of the cat has lost its danger.

14. Laurence Stapleton in "Neatness of Finish!" cites Williams's *Kora in Hell* and his scorn for art "carefully wrapped in brown paper and sent to a publisher" or a "bouquet frozen in an ice-cake" (16). For him, this is "Neatness and finish; the dust out of every corner" (*Imaginations*, 71). But Moore's source is also Ruskin, talking of "Giotto's genius." It "came into the world," he says, "exactly at the time when its rapidity of invention was not likely to be hampered by demands for imitative dexterity or neatness of finish" (Review of Lord Lindsay's *History of Christian Art* (1847), as quoted by Fiona Green, "'An Octopus' and National Character," in *Critics and Poets on Marianne Moore*, ed. Leavell, 147).

15. Williams, "Marianne Moore" (1948), 125–127.

16. Eliot, "East Coker" II and III. "The poetry does not matter. / It was not (to start again) what one had expected. . . . You say I am repeating / Something I had said before. I shall say it again."

17. Koch, "The Peaceable Kingdom of Marianne Moore."

18. Moore later omitted the Audubon reference, but it appears in the original published version which belongs to the sequence "Part of a Novel, Part of a Poem, Part of a Play."

19. Just before reading "The Steeple-Jack" at Amherst College, 10 May 1956, Moore remarks: "The most of my pieces of verse—you notice I don't say 'poems': I don't think they are that—are based on some incident, something that interested me, and there were eight beached whales in Long Island Sound or south of Brooklyn somewhere at the time I was writing this." The unpublished recording is in the Amherst College archives. See Slatin, *The Savage's Romance*, 181, for an account of the whale missed by Dürer.

20. Dürer's *Landscape*, in the possession of the Ashmolean Museum since 1855, was probably seen by Moore when she visited Oxford in 1910: that is, before the New York exhibition of Dürer prints in 1928 and her description of "a small Turner-like watercolor of the Tyrol in the Ashmolean" (*Dial* 85 (July 1928), reprinted in *Complete Prose*, 203).

21 Slatin, *The Savage's Romance*, 192.

22. Hoover—"one of our great men" (Moore, *Selected Letters*, 299) and in the ranks of history's finest figures, according to her unpublished 1932 poem "A Patriot"—is mentioned in her draft letter to George Saintsbury, 7 August 1930: "The temperature in Washington where our sin-driven senators have had to be kept in after school by Mr Hoover, is 104" (unpublished typescript, Rosenbach Museum and Library). Hoover had specially convened Congress in July 1930 for the ratification of the London Naval Disarmament Treaty.

23. Studio recording at the City College, New York, 14 February 1941. The unpublished recording is in the City University archives. Moore also changes "could not" to "scarcely could" in her reading at San Francisco State University, 10 October 1957, published by the San Francisco State University Poetry Center.

CHAPTER SIX   Quick, Said the Bird

1. Eliot, *The Use of Poetry and the Use of Criticism*, 118–119.

2. Williams, letter to Moore, 2 June 1932 (*Selected Letters*, 122–123): "The first one especially ["The Steeple-Jack" in the June 1932 sequence of three poems in *Poetry*] is reward enough for any waiting. [Moore had not published a new poem for seven years.] . . . And to me especially you give me a sense of triumph in that it is my own scene without mistaking the local for the parochial."

3. "I can't stop to indicate who is saying what, but Mr. Sweeney is saying most of what's of any importance. This was a work I never finished because it has to be spoken too quickly to be possible on the stage, to convey the sort of rhythm that I intended": Eliot's remarks during a poetry reading at Columbia University, 28 April 1958. His commentary was published in *Columbia University Forum* 2.1 (Fall 1958), 11–14. Note the manic speed with which he reads the poem for the Harvard Poetry Room in 1947.

4. North, *The Dialect of Modernism*, 90.

5. Ibid., 88.

6. Eliot, "From Poe to Valéry," reprinted in *To Criticize the Critic*, 31. However, the "living dead" aspect of Poe's tales clearly took imaginative possession of him in "The Death of St. Narcissus" (c.1914) as suggested by Grover Smith, "Eliot and the Ghost of Poe."

7. Eliot, "From Poe to Valéry," reprinted in *To Criticize the Critic*, 31.

8. Eliot, "'A Dream within a Dream,'" 244.

9. See Helen Gardner on "emphatic rhythms," *The Art of T. S. Eliot*, 34: "Mr. Eliot has never been one to despise a 'good tune.' When he selected a group of poems to be broadcast by the BBC in 1947 [*Poetry Anthology*, BBC Third Programme, 13 November 1947, read by John Laurie]—not his favourite poems, but poems that stayed in his head . . . —it was noticeable that after Johnson's 'Elegy on Dr. Robert Levett,' all the poems he chose, with the exception of Shelley's 'Art thou pale for weariness,' were 'thumpers': Scott's 'Bonny Dundee,' Poe's 'For Annie,' Kipling's 'Danny Deever,' Davidson's 'Thirty Bob a Week.'"

10. Steven Feld, "Waterfalls of Song," 91ff.

11. The particular song quoted in "Waterfalls of Song," 117–118, features the hooded butcherbird

perching in the large *sal* tree at Wafeyo hill
calling in the *uf* [another big hardwood tree]
calling from the close-by *haido* [a large palm]
calling in the *uf* there

12. See the original draft of *Ash-Wednesday*, King's College archive, Cambridge University; the recording in the Sound Recording Archives of Bowling Green State University of George Moran and Charles Mack's "Two Black Birds" routine; Susan Clement, "'All Aboard for Natchez, Cairo and St. Louis': The Source of a Draft Heading of T. S. Eliot's *Ash-Wednesday*"; and the chapter by Schuchard, "All Aboard for Natchez, Cairo and St. Louis: The Journey of the Exile in *Ash-Wednesday*," in *Eliot's Dark Angel*, 148–161.

13. I. A. Richards remembers Eliot's "delighted and highly critical immersion in records of 'The Two Black Crows,' especially of a record involving, 'All aboard for St. Louis.' I don't know how often we were patiently taught how to say this right" (quoted by Schuchard, *Eliot's Dark Angel*, 148).

14. Williams, "The Fatal Blunder," 125–126: "When [Eliot] says a thing like that we know that he must be either mad or asleep . . . We live only in one place at a time but far from being bound by it, only through it do we realize our freedom."

15. Eliot, preface to *This American World* by Edgar Ansel Mowrer, xiv.

16. As indicated by an early draft (Bodleian MS. Don.c23 [1]) which connects the woodthrush in the fog to Rogue Island, and hence to the bay where Eliot sailed as a boy.

17. In Rudyard Kipling's 1903 story "They," an American looking for somewhere to live in southern England chances upon a Tudor house where he hears "between . . . two notes" of doves on the roof "the utterly happy chuckle of a child"—though a dead one—"absorbed in some light mischief" (*Traffics and Discoveries*, 305). Another child, J. M. Barrie's Mary Rose, in the 1919 play of that name, would also seem to be a literary antecedent for the other "Little Gidding" hidden "children in the apple-tree." Before she

vanishes into an ageless realm, she is only a voice inside the apple tree which, says a stage direction for act 1, is "in full blossom at the open window" of her parents' living room (*The Plays of J. M. Barrie*, 544).

18. Eliot, "The Influence of Landscape upon the Poet," 421.

19. See also the contrast between cultivated fruit and Chinese ceramic versions in "Nine Nectarines," discussed by Robin G. Schulze, "Marianne Moore's 'Imperious Ox, Imperial Dish' and the Poetry of the Natural World," 1–33.

20. Moore, letter to Eliot, 12 March 1935, *Selected Letters*, 343: "[T]he originality in tempo (especially of "New Hampshire") and your indigeneous rhythm ought to be a great pleasure to you." Quoting "Virginia," she is reminded of the background to her forthcoming poems, "Virginia Britannia" and "Smooth Gnarled Crape Myrtle," because the quotation "brings back to me last summer and my brother's lawn bordered by crepe myrtle trees, and visited by the mocking-bird."

21. "Dans *Ulalume*, par exemple, et dans *Un Coup de Dés*, cette incantation, qui insiste sur la puissance primitive du mot (*Fatum*) est manifeste" ("Note Sur Mallarmé et Poe," 524–526).

22. *Fatum* as Destiny is important for Eliot when he describes Virgil's Aeneas as the servant of a higher power whose maintenance of continuity between ancient Rome and Christendom gives meaning to history ("Virgil and the Christian World," BBC Third Programme, 9 September 1951; published in *On Poetry and Poets*, 128).

23. Eliot, "Note Sur Mallarmé et Poe," 526: "Il y à aussi la fermeté de leur pas lorsqu'ils passent du monde tangible au mode dès fantômes." See also the later relevance to "Little Gidding" in Christopher Ricks, "A Note on 'Little Gidding.'"

24. Writing to John Hayward on 22 September 1941 about a change he had made in a draft of "Little Gidding"—so that "We strode together in a dead patrol" is replaced by "We trod the pavement in a dead patrol"—Eliot says that "a reminder of the surface of the Cromwell Road is timely" (Helen Gardner, *The Composition of* Four Quartets, 181).

25. "Cape Ann" was privately printed in October 1935, together with "Usk," under the title *Two Poems*, for Eliot to give away that Christmas, in particular to Emily Hale. In that sense, it was "written on the eve of Emily's departure from England in December 1935" (Lyndall Gordon, *Eliot's New Life*, 158). Like "Usk," which resulted from a July 1935 visit to Wales, it postdates "Burnt Norton," written shortly after Easter 1935.

26. Chapman, *Handbook of Birds of Eastern North America*, 245. See also Dean Flower, "Thrush Music, Audubon, and the Birds of America," *Hudson Review* 53.3 (2000), 505–512.

27. The 28 April 1933 reading at Bryn Mawr was reported in the *College News*, 3 May 1933, 1 and 3.

28. Unlike later printings, the version of "Cape Ann" that appeared in *Two Poems*, *New Democracy* (15 December 1935) and *Collected Poems 1909–1935* had no space before the last line, "The palaver is finished." Eliot's later insertion of a space is described by Christopher Ricks (who notes the Portuguese origin of "palaver" in *palavra*, "a talk or colloquy with the natives") as "the separation-off of anything to do with 'palaver' from all the other sounds, the bird-sounds that have been sounded in the poem and the verse-sounds themselves, the delight in obvious rhymes and unmisgiving assonances and alliterations" (*Decisions and Revisions in T. S. Eliot*, 90).

29. Eliot, *After Strange Gods*, 16–17.

30. Duncan observes how the stalwart gestures of Moore's later verse hark back to her earlier poetic manner. She can still "be aroused to display her backbone, to bristle her armatures" ("Ideas of the Meaning of Form," 30).

31. Insisting, "with a large NO," during her 1 May 1964 reading at Harvard, that she will not be reading "Melanchthon," the title she had given to "Black Earth"—"Everyone misunderstands it"—Moore goes on to say, "Now this is a better one" and reads "Elephants" instead. Unpublished recording in the Woodberry Poetry Room, Harvard University.

32. Typescript draft (A194) in the Poetry Collection of Manuscripts, State University of New York, Buffalo: "but at the last moment / just before alighting . . ."

33. Williams, reading at the 92nd Street YM-YWHA Poetry Center, New York, 27 January 1954, *Collected Recordings*.

CHAPTER SEVEN   A Way to the Last Leaftip

1. Williams, reading for Kenneth Burke, 21 June 1951, *Collected Recordings*.

2. Williams, reading at Harvard University, 18 June 1951 (Woodberry Poetry Room archive).

3. Typescript, Yale Collection, ZA Williams.

4. Ihde, *Listening and Voice*, 85.

5. Peter Quartermain, "Sound Reading," in *Close Listening*, 222.

6. Phlébas, le Phénicien, pendant quinze jours noyé,
   Oubliait les cris des mouettes et la houle de Cornouaille,
   Et les profits et les pertes, et la cargaison d'étain:
   Un courant de sous-mer l'emporta très loin,
   Le repassant aux étapes de sa vie antérieure.
   Figurez-vous donc, c'était un sort pénible;
   Cependant, ce fut jadis un bel homme, de haute taille. (CPP, 51)

7. The lines on Phlebas in *The Waste Land* are now part of a third and final sequence. After their first appearance in "Dans Le Restaurant," they had appeared next in a revised and translated form at the end of the long draft version, "Death by Water." (See *The Waste Land: A Facsimile and Transcript of the Original Drafts, including the Annotations of Ezra Pound*, ed. Valerie Eliot, 55–61.) It as if Eliot, having removed them from their French origin, has kept the sea change, but now imagines a second "foreign" cleansing and metamorphosis in a passage that journeys beyond America and its fishing grounds ("We beat around the cape" [Cape Cod] "and laid our course / From the Dry Salvages to the eastern banks") before coming to an end in Arctic disaster like Poe's Arthur Gordon Pym. The escape from an American association parallels Eliot's cancellation of the Boston revelers' passage in the original version of "The Burial of the Dead" (*Facsimile and Transcript*, 5).

8. "Chapter I," *Spring and All*, in *Collected Poems I: 1909–1939*, 185.

9. Writing to Williams, 7 July 1957, on the impending publication of his *Selected Letters*, Moore says: "I trust not *too* much space is devoted to American vs. English—about which we congenitally differ, do we not?" (Moore, *Selected Letters*, 539).

10. Not directly from James, it would seem (as in the 1913 *A Small Boy and Others* where Henry and William were "accessible to experience," *Autobiography*, 125), but, as Jeredith Merrin points out, from Dixon Scott's 1917 *Man of Letters*: "All [Henry James the elder] cared to produce was that condition of character which his son calls 'accessibility to experience'" ("Sites of Struggle: Marianne Moore and American Calvinism" in *The Calvinist Roots of the Modern Era*, ed. Barnstone, 102).

11. See Williams's letter to Horace Gregory, 5 May 1944, *Selected Letters*, 224: "In a discussion of local and general culture, [Eliot] is a maimed man. But of recent years I have noticed that he is trying to get down to the local again, trying to find his youth." In a letter to James Laughlin, 9 December 1942, Williams already thought that Eliot's essay of the same year, "The Music of Poetry," showed a new regard for the importance of place (*William Carlos Williams and James Laughlin: Selected Letters*, 80).

SELECTED BIBLIOGRAPHY

Works by Williams, Eliot, and Moore

WILLIAMS

The Autobiography of William Carlos Williams. New York: New Directions, 1967.

"Belly Music." *Others* 5.6 (July 1919): 25–32.

"By the Road to the Contagious Hospital." *Broom* (November 1923): 208.

The Collected Poems of William Carlos Williams I, 1909–1939. Edited by A. Walton Litz and Christopher MacGowan. New York: New Directions, 1986.

The Collected Poems of William Carlos Williams II, 1939–1962. Edited by Christopher MacGowan. New York: New Directions, 1988.

"The Comic Life of Elia Brobitza." *Others* 5.5 (April–May 1919): 1–16.

"The Fatal Blunder." *Quarterly Review of Literature* 2.2 (1945): 125–126.

I Wanted to Write a Poem: The Autobiography of the Works of a Poet. Edited by Edith Heal. New York: New Directions, 1978.

Imaginations. Edited by Webster Schott. New York: New Directions, 1971.

In the American Grain: Essays by William Carlos Williams. New York: New Directions, 1956.

Introduction to Moore's "Those Various Scalpels" and "In the Days of Prismatic Color." *Contact* 2 (January 1921): 1.

Many Loves and Other Plays: The Collected Plays of William Carlos Williams. Norfolk, CT: New Directions, 1961.

"Marianne Moore" (1925). In Williams, *Imaginations*, 310–320.

"Marianne Moore" (1948). *Quarterly Review of Literature* 4.2 (1948): 125–127.

Paterson. Revised edition. Edited by Christopher MacGowan. New York: New Directions, 1992.

"Robert McAlmon's Prose (I)." *Transatlantic Review* 1.5 (May 1924): 361–364.

"Sample Prose Piece: The Three Letters." *Contact* 4 (Summer 1921): 10–13.

The Selected Letters of William Carlos Williams. Edited by John C. Thirlwall. New York: McDowell, Obolensky, 1957.

Selected Poems. Edited by Charles Tomlinson. Harmondsworth, England: Penguin Books, 1983.

"Tract." *Others* 2.2 (February 1916): 139.

The Wedge. Cummington, MA: Cummington Press, 1944.

William Carlos Williams and James Laughlin: Selected Letters. Edited by Hugh Witemeyer. New York: W. W. Norton, 1989.

William Carlos Williams: The Collected Recordings. Keele, UK: Keele University, 1992, 1993. Published online by PennSound (University of Pennsylvania), 2007. http://writing.upenn.edu/pennsound/

Yes, Mrs. Williams: A Personal Record of My Mother. New York: New Directions, 1982.

ELIOT

After Strange Gods: A Primer of Modern Heresy. London: Faber and Faber, 1934.
"American Literature." *Athenaeum* 4643 (25 April 1919): 23.
"'A Dream within a Dream': Edgar Allan Poe." *Listener* 29 (25 February 1943): 243–244.
"The Influence of Landscape upon the Poet." *Daedalus: Journal of the American Academy of Arts and Sciences* 89.2 (Spring 1960): 421.
Inventions of the March Hare: Poems 1909–1917. Edited by Christopher Ricks. London: Faber and Faber, 1996.
The Letters of T. S. Eliot, I, 1898–1922. Edited by Valerie Eliot. London: Faber and Faber, 1988.
"Mr. Lee Masters." *Manchester Guardian* (9 October 1916): 3.
"Note Sur Mallarmé et Poe." *Nouvelle Revue Française* 27 (July–December 1926): 524–526.
On Poetry and Poets. London: Faber and Faber, 1957.
"The Preacher as Artist." *Athenaeum* 4674 (28 November 1919): 1252.
Preface to *This American World*, by Edgar Ansel Mowrer, ix–xv.
"Reflections on Contemporary Poetry." *Egoist* 6 (July 1919): 40.
Review of *Poems* and *Marriage*, by Marianne Moore. *Dial* 75 (December 1923): 594–597.
Selected Essays. London: Faber and Faber, 1969.
Selected Prose. Edited by John Hayward. Harmondsworth, England: Penguin Books, 1953.
"T. S. Eliot Talks About His Poetry." *Columbia University Forum* 2.1 (Fall 1958): 11–14.
T. S. Eliot: The Complete Poems and Plays. London: Faber and Faber, 1969.
To Criticize the Critic and Other Writings. London: Faber and Faber, 1965.
The Use of Poetry and the Use of Criticism. London: Faber and Faber, 1964.
The Waste Land: A Facsimile and Transcript of the Original Drafts. Edited by Valerie Eliot. London: Faber and Faber, 1971.
The Waste Land. Read by the author. Columbia University, May 1933. Published online by the Poetry Archive. http://www.poetryarchive.org/poetryarchive/singlePoem.do?poemId=7630 (accessed 6 June 2011).
The Waste Land. Read by the author. NBC Studios, New York, 26 July 1946. The Library of Congress and HarperAudio.

MOORE

Becoming Marianne Moore: The Early Poems, 1907–1924. Edited by Robin G. Schulze. Berkeley: University of California Press, 2002.
"Black Earth." *Egoist* 4.5 (April 1918): 55–56.
The Complete Prose of Marianne Moore. Edited by Patricia C. Willis. New York: Viking, 1987.
"Critics and Connoisseurs." *Others* 3.1 (July 1916): 4–5.
"English Literature since 1914." *Marianne Moore Newsletter* 4 (Fall 1980): 13.
"The Fish." *Egoist* 7.5 (August 1918): 95.
"'He Wrote the History Book,' It Said." *Egoist* 5.3 (1 May 1916): 53.

"In the Days of Prismatic Colour." Byrn Mawr *Lantern* 27 (Spring 1919): 35.

"In This Age of Hard Trying, Nonchalance is Good and." *Chimaera* 1.2 (July 1916): 52–53.

Marianne Moore: Complete Poems. London: Faber and Faber, 1968.

Marianne Moore: Selected Poems. London: Faber and Faber, 1969.

Observations. New York: Dial Press, 1924.

"Part of a Novel, Part of a Poem, Part of a Play." *Poetry* 40.3 (June 1932): 119–128.

The Poems of Marianne Moore. Edited by Grace Schulman. London: Viking, 2003.

The Selected Letters of Marianne Moore. Edited by Bonnie Costello, Celeste Goodridge, and Cristanne Miller. London: Faber and Faber, 1998.

"The Steeple-Jack." In Moore, "Part of a Novel, Part of a Poem, Part of a Play," 119–127.

"Those Various Scalpels." Byrn Mawr *Lantern* 25 (Spring 1917): 50–51.

"To a Man Working His Way Through the Crowd." *Egoist* 4.2 (April 1915): 62.

"To Bernard Shaw: A Prize Bird." *Egoist* 8.2 (2 August 1915): 126.

"To Disraeli on Conservatism." Bryn Mawr *Lantern* 23 (Spring 1915): 60.

"To Statecraft Embalmed." *Others* 1.6 (December 1915): 104.

"To the Soul of 'Progress.'" *Egoist* 4.2 (1 April 1915): 62.

Critical and Other Works on Williams, Eliot, and Moore

Aimé-Martin, Louis, ed. *Lettres édifiantes et curieuses concernant l'Asie, l'Afrique et l'Amérique.* Paris: Panthéon Litteraire, 1843.

Bagchee, Shyamal, ed. *T. S. Eliot: A Voice Descanting: Centenary Essays.* London: Macmillan, 1990.

Baker, Houston A., Jr. *Modernism and the Harlem Renaissance.* Chicago: University of Chicago Press, 1987.

Barnstone, Aliki, Michael Tomasek Manson, and Carol J. Singley, eds. *The Calvinist Roots of the Modern Era.* Hanover, NH: University Press of New England, 1997.

Barrie, J. M. *The Plays of J. M. Barrie.* London: Hodder and Stoughton, 1928.

Baxter, Richard. *The Saint's Everlasting Rest or a Treatise of the Blessed State of the Saints in Heaven.* Edited by William Brown. Edinburgh, 1838.

Bell, A. O., ed. Assisted by A. McNeillie. *The Diary of Virginia Woolf II, 1920–1924.* London: Hogarth Press, 1978.

Bernstein, Charles, ed. *Close Listening: Poetry and the Performed Word.* New York: Oxford University Press, 1998.

Bishop, Elizabeth. "Efforts of Affection: A Memoir of Marianne Moore." In *Elizabeth Bishop: The Collected Prose,* edited by Robert Giroux, 121–156. New York: Farrar, Straus and Giroux, 1986.

Bronk, William. *Life Supports: New and Collected Poems.* Jersey City: Talisman House Publishers, 1981.

Cather, Willa. "New Types of Acting." *McClure's Magazine* (February 1914): 42.

Chapman, Frank M. *Handbook of Birds of Eastern North America.* 1886. Reprint, New York: Dover, 1966.

Chappell, Charles. "Botched Romantic Strategy in Williams' 'Portrait of a Lady.'" *William Carlos Williams Review* 15.1 (Spring 1987): 41–47.

Clement, Susan. "'All Aboard for Natchez, Cairo and St. Louis': The Source of a Draft

Heading of T. S. Eliot's *Ash-Wednesday.*" *Notes and Queries* 241 (March 1996): 57–59.

Connor, Steven. *Dumbstruck: A Cultural History of Ventriloquism.* Oxford: Oxford University Press, 2001.

Conrad, Bryce. *Refiguring America: A Study of William Carlos Williams' In the American Grain.* Urbana: University of Illinois Press, 1990.

Costello, Bonnie. *Marianne Moore: Imaginary Possessions.* Cambridge, MA: Harvard University Press, 1981.

Craig, Edward Gordon. *On the Art of the Theatre.* London: Heinemann, 1914.

———. *Towards a New Theatre: Forty Designs for Stage Scenes, with Critical Notes.* London: Dent, 1913.

Creeley, Robert, ed. *Selected Writings of Charles Olson.* New York: New Directions, 1966.

Cushman, Stephen. *William Carlos Williams and the Meaning of Measure.* New Haven: Yale University Press, 1985.

Dijkstra, Bram. *The Hieroglyphics of a New Speech: Cubism, Stieglitz, and the Early Poetry of William Carlos Williams.* Princeton, NJ: Princeton University Press, 1966.

Duncan, Robert. "Ideas of the Meaning of Form." 1961. In *A Selected Prose* by Robert Duncan, edited by Robert J. Bertholf, 30. New York: New Directions, 1995.

Eliot, George. *Daniel Deronda.* Harmondsworth, UK: Penguin, 1977.

Emerson, Ralph Waldo. *The Works of Ralph Waldo Emerson: Poems.* Vol. 5. London: Bell, 1914.

Fairman, Charles E. *Art and Artists of the Capitol of the United States of America.* Washington, DC: United States Government Printing Office, 1927.

Feld, Steven. "Waterfalls of Song: An Acoustemology of Place Resounding in Bosavi, Papua New Guinea." In *Senses of Place,* edited by Steven Feld and Keith H. Basso, 91ff. Santa Fe: School of American Research, 1996.

Fellowes, E. H. *English Madrigal Verse 1588–1632: Edited from the Original Song Books.* 1919. Reprint, Oxford: Clarendon Press, 1929.

Gallup, Donald. *T. S. Eliot: A Bibliography.* London: Faber and Faber, 1969.

Gardner, Helen. *The Art of T. S. Eliot.* London: Cresset Press, 1949.

———. *The Composition of* Four Quartets. London: Faber and Faber, 1978.

Gassner, John. *Best Plays of the Early American Theatre: From the Beginning to 1916.* New York: Crown Publishers, 1967.

Gordon, Lyndall. *Eliot's Early Years.* London: Oxford University Press, 1977.

———. *Eliot's New Life.* Oxford: Oxford University Press, 1988.

Griffiths, Eric. *The Printed Voice of Victorian Poetry.* Oxford: Clarendon Press, 1989.

Hall, Donald. "Marianne Moore." In *Writers at Work: The* Paris Review *Interviews,* second series, edited by George Plimpton, 55–76. London: Secker and Warburg, 1963.

Halter, Peter. *The Revolution in the Visual Arts and the Poetry of William Carlos Williams.* Cambridge: Cambridge University Press, 1994.

Hardy, Thomas. *The Collected Poems of Thomas Hardy.* London: Macmillan, 1968.

Hartley, Marsden. *Adventures in the Arts: Informal Chapters on Painters, Vaudeville, and Poets.* 1921. Reprint, New York: Hacker Art Books, 1972.

Hatlen, Burton, and Demetres Tryphonopoulos, eds. *William Carlos Williams and the Language of Poetry.* Orono, ME: National Poetry Foundation, 2002.

Holley, Margaret. *The Poetry of Marianne Moore: A Study in Voice and Value.* Cambridge: Cambridge University Press, 1987.

Ihde, Don. *Listening and Voice: Phenomenologies of Sound.* Revised edition. Albany: State University of New York Press, 2007.

James, Henry. *Autobiography.* Edited by F. W. Dupee. London: W. H. Allen, 1956.

———. *The Question of Our Speech/The Lesson of Balzac.* 1905. Reprint, New York: Haskell House, 1972.

Jepson, Edgar. "The Western School." *Little Review* 5 (September 1918): 9.

Kahn, Douglas. *Noise, Water, Meat: A History of Sound in the Arts.* Cambridge, MA: MIT Press, 2001.

Kearns, Cleo McNelly. *T. S. Eliot and Indic Traditions: A Study in Poetry and Belief.* Cambridge: Cambridge University Press, 1987.

Kennedy, X. J. *An Introduction to Poetry.* Boston: Little, Brown, 1966.

Kipling, Rudyard. *Traffics and Discoveries.* London: Macmillan, 1904.

Koch, Vivienne. "The Peaceable Kingdom of Marianne Moore." *Quarterly Review of Literature* 4.2 (1948): 219.

Kyd, Thomas. *The Spanish Tragedy.* In *Six Renaissance Tragedies*, edited by Colin Gibson. Basingstoke, UK: Macmillan, 1997.

Lawrence, D. H. *Phoenix: The Posthumous Papers of D. H. Lawrence.* Edited by Edward D. McDonald. London: Heinemann, 1961.

———. *Studies in Classic American Literature.* London: Heinemann, 1964.

Layng, George W. "Rephrasing Whitman, Williams and the Visual Idiom." In Hatlen, *William Carlos Williams and the Language of Poetry*, 183.

Leavell, Linda, Cristanne Miller, and Robin G. Schulze, eds. *Critics and Poets on Marianne Moore: "A Right Good Salvo of Barks."* Lewisburg, PA: Bucknell University Press, 2005.

Levy, Ellen. "Natural Reticence: Editing Marianne Moore." *Literary Imagination* 12.2 (2010): 237.

Lindsay, Vachel. *The Congo and Other Poems.* New York: Macmillan, 1914.

MacGowan, Christopher. *William Carlos Williams's Early Poetry: The Visual Arts Background.* Ann Arbor: UMI Research Press, 1984.

Mariani, Paul. *William Carlos Williams: A New World Naked.* New York: W. W. Norton, 1990.

McAlmon, Robert. *A Hasty Bunch.* 1922. Reprint, Carbondale: Southern Illinois University Press, 1977.

McCaffery, Steve. "Voice in Extremis." In Bernstein, *Close Listening: Poetry and the Performed Word*, 162–177.

Miller, J. Hillis. *The Linguistic Moment: From Wordsworth to Stevens.* Princeton, NJ: Princeton University Press, 1985.

Molesworth, Charles. *Marianne Moore: A Literary Life.* New York: Atheneum, 1990.

Moody, A. D. "T. S. Eliot: The American Strain." In *The Placing of T. S. Eliot*, edited by Jewel Spears Brooker, 77–89. Columbia: University of Missouri Press, 1991.

More, Paul Elmer. *Shelburne Essays, Ninth Series*. 1915. Reprint, New York: Phaeton, 1967.

Mowrer, Edgar Ansel. *This American World*. London: Faber and Gwyer, 1928.

North, Michael. *The Dialect of Modernism: Race, Language, and Twentieth-Century Literature*. New York: Oxford University Press, 1994.

Olson, Charles. *Projective Verse*. 1950. In Creeley, *Selected Writings of Charles Olson*, 22.

Ong, Walter J. *Orality and Literacy: The Technologizing of the Word*. London: Methuen, 1982.

Oser, Lee. *T. S. Eliot and American Poetry*. Columbia: University of Missouri Press, 1998.

Perloff, Marjorie. *The Poetics of Indeterminacy: Rimbaud to Cage*. Evanston, IL: Northwestern University Press, 1983.

———. "'To Give a Design': Williams and the Visualization of Poetry." In *William Carlos Williams: Man and Poet*, edited by Carroll F. Terrell, 159–186. Orono, ME: National Poetry Foundation, 1983.

———. *21st-Century Modernism: The "New" Poetics*. Malden, MA: Blackwell, 2002.

———, and Craig Dworkin, eds. *The Sound of Poetry/The Poetry of Sound*. Chicago: University of Chicago Press, 2009.

Perloff, Nancy. "Sound Poetry and the Musical Avant-Garde: A Musicologist's Perspective." In Marjorie Perloff, *The Sound of Poetry/The Poetry of Sound*, 97–117.

Picker, John M. *Victorian Soundscapes*. Oxford: Oxford University Press, 2003.

Plimpton, George, ed. *Writers at Work: The* Paris Review *Interviews*. London: Secker and Warburg, 1973.

Poe, Edgar Allan. *The Complete Works of Edgar Allan Poe*. Edited by James A. Harrison. New York: AMS Press, 1965.

Pound, Ezra. *The Selected Letters of Ezra Pound, 1907–1941*. Edited by D. D. Paige. London: Faber and Faber, 1971.

Quartermain, Peter. "Sound Reading." In Bernstein, *Close Listening: Poetry and the Performed Word*, 217–230.

Rée, Jonathan. *I See a Voice: Deafness, Language and the Senses—A Philosophical History*. New York: Henry Holt, 1999.

Rhodes, Geri M. "The Paterson Metaphor in William Carlos Williams's *Paterson*." Master's thesis, Tufts University, 1965.

Ricks, Christopher. *Decisions and Revisions in T. S. Eliot* (Panizzi Lectures). London: British Library and Faber and Faber, 2003.

———. "A Note on 'Little Gidding.'" *Essays in Criticism* 25–27 (January 1975): 145–153.

Rostand, Edmond. *Chantecler: Pièce en Quatre Actes, en vers*. Paris: Charpentier, 1910.

Sayre, Henry M. *The Visual Text of William Carlos Williams*. Urbana: University of Illinois Press, 1983.

Schuchard, Ronald. *Eliot's Dark Angel: Intersections of Life and Art*. New York: Oxford University Press, 1999.

Schulman, Grace. "A Conversation with Marianne Moore." *Quarterly Review of Literature* 16.12 (1969): 154–161.

———. *Marianne Moore: The Poetry of Engagement*. New York: Paragon House, 1989.

Schulze, Robin G. "Marianne Moore's 'Imperious Ox, Imperial Dish' and the Poetry of the Natural World." *Twentieth Century Literature* 44.1 (Spring 1998): 1–33.

Schweighauser, Philipp. *The Noises of American Literature, 1890–1985: Toward a History of Literary Acoustics*. Gainesville: University Press of Florida, 2006.

Shakespeare, William. *Cariolanus*. In *The Oxford Shakespeare: The Complete Works*, edited by Stanley Wells and Gary Taylor. Oxford: Clarendon Press, 1988.

———. *Richard II*. In *The Oxford Shakespeare: The Complete Works*, edited by Stanley Wells and Gary Taylor. Oxford: Clarendon Press, 1988.

Slatin, John M. "American Beauty: William Carlos Williams and Marianne Moore." In *WCW & Others: Essays on William Carlos Williams and His Association with Ezra Pound, Hilda Doolittle, Marcel Duchamp, Marianne Moore, Emanuel Romano, Wallace Stevens, and Louis Zukofsky*, edited by Dave Oliphant and Thomas Zigal, 61–81. Austin: Harry Ransom Humanities Research Center, University of Texas at Austin, 1985.

———. *The Savage's Romance: The Poetry of Marianne Moore*. University Park: Pennsylvania State University Press, 1986.

Smith, Bruce R. *The Acoustic World of Early Modern England: Attending to the O-Factor*. Chicago: University of Chicago Press, 1999.

Smith, Grover. "Eliot and the Ghost of Poe." In Bagchee, *T. S. Eliot: A Voice Descanting: Centenary Essays*, 149–163.

Smoller, Sanford J. *Adrift Among Geniuses: Robert McAlmon, Writer and Publisher of the Twenties*. University Park: Pennsylvania State University Press, 1975.

Stapleton, Laurence. "Neatness of Finish!" *Marianne Moore Newsletter* 1.2 (Fall 1977): 16.

Tate, Allen, ed. *T. S. Eliot: The Man and His Work*. London: Chatto and Windus, 1967.

Tomlinson, Charles. *Metamorphoses: Poetry and Translation*. Manchester: Carcanet Press, 2003.

———. *Charles Tomlinson Reads* The Waste Land *by T. S. Eliot*. Recorded 11 April 1989. Keele, UK: Keele University, 1989.

Toomer, Jean. *Cane*. Edited by Darwin T. Turner. 1923. Reprint, New York: W. W. Norton, 1988.

Tourneur, Cyril. *The Revenger's Tragedy*. London: Arnold, 1967.

Townley, Rod. *The Early Poetry of William Carlos Williams*. Ithaca: Cornell University Press, 1975.

Vescia, Monique Claire. *Depression Glass: Documentary Photography and the Medium of the Camera-Eye in Charles Reznikoff, George Oppen, and William Carlos Williams*. New York: Routledge, 2006.

Walker, David. *The Transparent Lyric: Reading and Meaning in the Poetry of Stevens and Williams*. Princeton, NJ: Princeton University Press, 1984.

Wallace, Emily Mitchell. *A Bibliography of William Carlos Williams*. Middletown, CT: Wesleyan University Press, 1968.

Weaver, Mike. *William Carlos Williams: The American Background*. Cambridge: Cambridge University Press, 1977.

Webster, John. *The White Devil*. Tonbridge, UK: Ernest Benn, 1984.

Whitman, Walt. *Complete Prose Works*. New York: Appleton, 1909.

———. *Leaves of Grass*. Edited by Jerome Loving. Oxford: Oxford University Press, 1990.

Willis, Patricia C. "Not of Any School." *Marianne Moore Newsletter* 2 (Spring 1978): 9–12.

SELECTED LIST OF RECORDED READINGS

WILLIAMS

9 January 1942. National Council of Teachers of English and Columbia University Press Contemporary Poets series. The Red Wheelbarrow. Tract. The Defective Record. A Coronal. To Elsie. The Wind Increases. Classic Scene.

5 May 1945. Library of Congress. Sonnet 1909 (Martin and Katherine). Paterson: The Falls. Peace on Earth. Postlude. Pastoral ("When I was younger"). Pastoral ("The little sparrows"). Dawn. Portrait of a Woman in Bed. Sympathetic Portrait of a Child. Spring Strains. Dedication for a Plot of Ground. Love Song ("I lie here thinking of you"). Overture to a Dance of Locomotives. Complaint. The Cold Night. Primrose. Queen-Anne's Lace. To a Friend Concerning Several Ladies. Youth and Beauty. The Thinker. The Nightingales. The Widow's Lament in Springtime. Light Hearted William. Spring and All. The Farmer. The Eyeglasses. Shoot it Jimmy! To Elsie. The Red Wheelbarrow. Rigamarole. It is a Living Coral. The Bull. The Botticellian Trees. Flowers by the Sea. The Yachts. The Term. A Sort of a Song. The Dance ("In Brueghel's great picture"). Burning the Christmas Greens. In Sisterly Fashion. The World Narrowed to a Point. The Hounded Lovers. The Cure. The Rose ("The stillness of the rose"). Perfection. The Last Turn. The Aftermath. The Yellow Chimney. Raleigh was Right. A Night in June (short story).

18 October 1947. Library of Congress. The Semblables. The Catholic Bells. Perpetuum Mobile: The City. Excerpts from Paterson II.iii, Paterson I.i, and Paterson I.iii.

20 May 1949. Columbia Records "Pleasure Dome" series. The Young Housewife. The Bull. Poem ("As the cat"). Lear. The Dance ("In Brueghel's great picture"). El Hombre.

June 1950. Interview with John W. Gerber and Readings, Rutherford. Danse Russe. This Is Just to Say. Ol' Bunk's Band. Portrait of a Lady. El Hombre.

August 1950. Reading for Richard Wirtz Emerson, Rutherford. Choral: The Pink Church. Portrait of a Lady. Tract. Pastoral ("The little sparrows"). A Poem for Norman Macleod. To Waken an Old Lady. The Red Wheelbarrow. This Is Just to Say. The Bull. Perpetuum Mobile: The City. Poem ("As the cat"). Danse Russe. The Widow's Lament in Springtime. The Dance ("In Brueghel's great picture"). Lear. Mama. New Mexico. The Lion. St. Francis Einstein of the Daffodils.

15 November 1950. University of California, Los Angeles. In Sisterly Fashion. The Dance ("In Brueghel's great picture"). Franklin Square. Raleigh was Right. At the Faucet of

June. The Universality of Things. Rigamarole. To Elsie. Spring and All. The Pot of Flowers. It Is a Living Coral. All the Fancy Things. Paterson: The Falls. Poem ("As the cat"). Between Walls.

16 November 1950. Reading for Eyvind Earle, San Fernando Valley, California. In Sisterly Fashion. Tract. Smell! Flowers by the Sea. The Poor. To Elsie. This Is Just to Say. Impromptu: The Suckers. All the Fancy Things. It Is a Living Coral. Young Sycamore. The Cod Head. The Bull. Poem ("As the cat").

18 June 1951. Harvard University. The Desert Music.

21 June 1951. Reading for Kenneth Burke, New Jersey. The Desert Music. The Cod Head. Burning the Christmas Greens. A Sort of a Song. Excerpt from Paterson I.iii. Tract. Après le Bain. Spring is Here Again, Sir. May 1st Tomorrow.

4 December 1951. Harvard University. A Marriage Ritual. Burning the Christmas Greens. The Visit. The Lion. Spring and All. This Is Just to Say. On Gay Wallpaper. Flowers by the Sea. To a Poor Old Woman. The Yachts. History. Virtue. Smell! Struggle of Wings. To Greet a Letter-Carrier. At the Bar. These. Perfection. Fertile. Chanson. Design for November. Picture of a Nude in a Machine Shop. The Hurricane. Venus over the Desert. The Birth of Venus.

19 March 1952. Princeton University. Portrait of a Lady. El Hombre. Tract. Pastoral ("The little sparrows"). Smell! Queen-Anne's-Lace. Waiting. The Hunter. Arrival. The Widow's Lament in Springtime. To Elsie. The Red Wheelbarrow. This Is Just to Say. Poem ("As the cat"). Flowers by the Sea. To a Poor Old Woman. The Catholic Bells. The Sea-Elephant. A Unison. The Desert Music.

16 May 1952. Hanover College, Indiana. Smell! Excerpt from Paterson II.ii. Portent. The Botticellian Trees. Flowers by the Sea. To a Mexican Pig-Bank. To a Poor Old Woman. Pastoral ("When I was younger"). To Elsie. On Gay Wallpaper.

27 January 1954. 92nd Street YM-YWHA Poetry Center, New York. A Sort of a Song. Burning the Christmas Greens. A Vision of Labor: 1931. The Yellow Chimney. Franklin Square. Labrador. The Apparition. The Maneuver. The Horse. The Act. Seafarer. The Three Graces. Paterson: Episode 17. Ol' Bunk's Band. A Unison. The Descent. The Yellow Flower. The Host. The Orchestra. Spring and All. Between Walls. On Gay Wallpaper. Fish.

6 June 1954. Caedmon Records, Rutherford. The Descent. To Daphne and Virginia. The Orchestra. For Eleanor and Bill Monahan. The Yellow Flower. The Host. Excerpts from Asphodel, That Greeny Flower. The Botticellian Trees. Flowers by the Sea. The Yachts. The Catholic Bells. Smell! Fish. Primrose. To Elsie. Between Walls. On Gay Wallpaper. The Red Lily. Seafarer.

19 May 1955. University of California, Berkeley. Spring and All. The Pot of Flowers. Rain. The Botticellian Trees. To a Mexican Pig-Bank. To A Poor Old Woman. The Catholic Bells. A Poem for Norman Macleod. Danse Russe. The Late Singer. At the

Faucet of June. The Avenue of Poplars. The Sun. A Sort of a Song. The Dance ("In Brueghel's great picture"). The Gentle Rejoinder. Seafarer. May 1st Tomorrow. A Unison. The Descent. To Daphne and Virginia. The Orchestra. Excerpt from Asphodel, That Greeny Flower.

May 1955. Reading for Eyvind Earle, San Fernando Valley, California. Peace on Earth. The Botticellian Trees. Flowers by the Sea. Primrose. Spring and All. On Gay Wallpaper. The Red Lily. The Sun. A Sort of a Song. May 1st Tomorrow. A Unison. The Descent. To Daphne and Virginia. The Orchestra. The Yellow Flower. The Host. The Mental Hospital Garden. Excerpt from Asphodel, That Greeny Flower. The Ivy Crown. Shadows. Excerpt from Asphodel, That Greeny Flower: Coda.

May 1955. University of California, Los Angeles. The Botticellian Trees. Flowers by the Sea. Primrose. Spring and All. To Elsie. On Gay Wallpaper. The Red Lily. The Sun. A Sort of a Song. Seafarer. May 1st Tomorrow. A Unison. The Sea-Elephant. The Descent. To Daphne and Virginia. The Orchestra. Shadows. Asphodel, that Greeny Flower: Coda.

ELIOT

1933. Harvard University Poetry Room. The Love Song of J. Alfred Prufrock. Gerontion. The Hollow Men. Triumphal March. Journey of the Magi. A Song for Simeon. Difficulties of a Statesman. Marina.

May 1933. Columbia University Recording Studio. Ash-Wednesday. Triumphal March. The Hollow Men. *The Waste Land.* Journey of the Magi. Marina. Sweeney among the Nightingales.

26 July 1946. Library of Congress (NBC Studios, New York). The Waste Land. Ash-Wednesday. New Hampshire. Virginia. Sweeney among the Nightingales. Coriolan. Difficulties of a Statesman. Whispers of Immortality.

October–November 1946. London. Burnt Norton (22 October). East Coker (12 November). The Dry Salvages (19 November). Little Gidding (28 November).

May 1947. Harvard Poetry Room. The Love Song of J. Alfred Prufrock. The Journey of the Magi. A Song for Simeon. Difficulties of a Statesman. Fragment of an Agon.

13 May 1947. Harvard University, Sanders Theater. Preludes. Morning at the Window. Sweeney among the Nightingales. "The Burial of the Dead" from *The Waste Land.* The Hollow Men. A Song for Simeon. Triumphal March. Landscapes. "Little Gidding" from *Four Quartets.*

23 May 1947. National Gallery of Art, Washington. The Love Song of J. Alfred Prufrock. La Figlia che Piange. Sweeney among the Nightingales. "What the Thunder Said" from *The Waste Land.* Journey of the Magi. Animula. Landscapes. *Ash-Wednesday.*

1948. Columbia University. The Love Song of J. Alfred Prufrock. Rhapsody on a Windy Night. The Hippopotamus. "A Game of Chess" and "What the Thunder Said" from *The Waste Land.* Readings from *Old Possum's Book of Practical Cats.* Fragment of an Agon. *Ash-Wednesday.* Lines for an Old Man.

November 1950. University of Chicago. Preludes. Journey of the Magi. "Death by Water" and "What the Thunder Said" from *The Waste Land.* Four Landscapes. "Little Gidding" from *Four Quartets.*

4 December 1950. 92nd Street YM-YWHA Poetry Center, New York. The Love Song of J. Alfred Prufrock. Preludes. La Figlia che Piange. Whispers of Immortality. Sweeney Erect. "The Burial of the Dead" and "What the Thunder Said" from *The Waste Land.* Coriolan. Triumphal March. Difficulties of a Statesman.

September 1955. Caedmon Records, London. Coriolan. Triumphal March. Marina. Chorus from *The Rock.* A Song for Simeon. *Ash-Wednesday.* Mr. Eliot's Sunday Morning Service. Preludes. The Love Song of J. Alfred Prufrock.

MOORE

14 February 1941. City College, New York. Sonnet 29 (Shakespeare). Virginia Britannia. Silence. The Bricks are Fallen Down.

January 1942. National Council of Teachers of English and Columbia University Press Contemporary Poets series. He "Digesteth Harde Yron." See in the Midst of Fair Leaves. The Buffalo. What Are Years?

7 November 1951. Readings for the Yale Historical Recordings Archive, New York. What Are Years? The Mind Is an Enchanting Thing. Voracities and Verities. Nevertheless. The Wood-Weasel. Propriety. Spenser's Ireland. Armor's Undermining Modesty. In Distrust of Merits.

1953. Caedmon Records. The Fish. To a Steam Roller. Spenser's Ireland. The Wood-Weasel. A Carriage from Sweden. The Mind Is an Enchanting Thing. Nine Nectarines. Armor's Undermining Modesty. Rigorists. A Face. Propriety. What Are Years? Readings from her translations of La Fontaine's *Fables.*

10 May 1956. Amherst College. I May, I Might, I Must. The Steeple-Jack. Bowls. The Jerboa. What Are Years? Nevertheless. The Mind Is an Enchanting Thing. A Face. The Sycamore. Readings from her translations of La Fontaine's *Fables.* Bird-Witted. Poetry.

18 October 1956. University of California, Berkeley. To a Chameleon. A Face. Nine Nectarines. When I Buy Pictures. A Carriage from Sweden. Propriety. Armor's Undermining Modesty. In Distrust of Merits. The Labors of Hercules. Values in Use. What Are Years? Silence. Readings from her translations of La Fontaine's *Fables.* Nevertheless.

10 October 1957. San Francisco State University. The Steeple-Jack. The Hero. The Jelly-Fish. The Labors of Hercules. Light Is Speech. He "Digesteth Harde Yron." Marriage (excerpts). His Shield. Values in Use. Hometown Piece for Messrs. Alston and Reese. The Fox and the Crow (La Fontaine). Poetry. In Distrust of Merits.

c. 1958 / 1959. WEVD Radio. The Wood-Weasel. His Shield. The Plumet Basilisk. O To Be a Dragon. A Grave. The Arctic Ox (or Goat). Four Quartz Crystal Clocks. Nine Nectarines. A Face.

6 November 1959. Readings for the Yale Historical Recordings Archive, New York. The Arctic Ox (or Goat). Saint Nicholas. Leonardo Da Vinci's. Marriage. Blessed is the Man. Apparition of Splendor. Logic and the Magic Flute. No Better than a Withered Daffodil. Bird-Witted. Efforts of Affection. The Frigate Pelican. The Plumet Basilisk. His Shield. In This Age of Hard Trying. The Pangolin. A Jellyfish. To a Chameleon. O To Be a Dragon. Melchior Vulpius.

1 May 1964. Harvard University. A Carriage from Sweden. An Expedient—Leonardo Da Vinci's—And a Query. He "Digesteth Harde Yron." Arthur Mitchell. To the Peacock of France. Elephants. W. S. Landor.

11 May 1965. Harvard University. In Lieu of the Lyre. The Jerboa. He "Digesteth Harde Yron." To a Snail. Arthur Mitchell. To a Giraffe. Tell Me, Tell Me. Leonardo Da Vinci's. Novices. What Are Years? The Mind Is an Enchanting Thing.

2 May 1968. University of Texas. Dream. A Face. The Mind Is an Enchanting Thing. To a Giraffe. What Are Years? Sun. Tell Me, Tell Me. "Avec Ardeur." O To Be a Dragon. The Lion in Love (La Fontaine).

PERMISSIONS

INDEX